What People Are Saying about Tiiu Napp and This Book

"Tiiu is 'love, pure love.' She is such a sweet, kind person with a heart of gold. In this book, she will help you step into the beautiful person you truly have within you. I love her positive spirit. She has lived what she shares in this book. Tiiu is a survivor. Her stories will give you hope. Enjoy the book and know that Tiiu is a person who is able and willing to guide you through the steps to get out of any situation that is not a good one for you."

— Mary West, Founder of The Mary West Network

"Tiiu Napp has more boldness in her pinkie than most people have in their whole body. When you see her *Eye of the Tiger* look, that means Tiiu is about to do something outrageously bold. Tiiu Napp, as importantly as being bold, carries within her a depth of wisdom and kindness coming from her fascinating experiences. She is a wise, bold, woman, a woman undeterred by mere obstacles."

— Bob Ingram, Author of *The Genius Who Saved Baseball*

"Raw and real...Tiiu doesn't hold anything back here. She's an inspiration and her chilling story is a must-read."

— Henry Klauke, Author of *Inbox Income*

"The book you hold in your hand, or are browsing and considering whether or not to buy, will be an investment in you and in your destiny. If you have suffered abuse, and many of us have in one form or another, then you need to dive into Tiiu's story of digging her way out of the miry clay of abuse and neglect, elevating her own life and destiny to new heights she never thought possible until she stepped on the road to healing the holes in her soul, so that she could rise above the abuse she suffered into a place of all consuming love. Simply put, you need this book and something led you to it; now follow through and buy it. Tiiu, well done and your book's accolades are well deserved."

— Dr. Shaun A. Sullivan, Author of *Head for Leading, Heart for Loving: Leveraging Influence, Compassion, and Relationships to Achieve Your Organizational Goals*

"The emotion and passion that Tiiu has infused into these pages brings her readers insight that is both timely and timeless. She provides experience and resources to help you become better equipped for the trials and tribulations of this adventure we call life."

— David Muller, Ultimate Achievers Alliance

"Tiiu Napp has suffered some truly difficult traumas and found ways to keep fighting for herself, for her spirit. *Healing the Holes in Your Soul* not only tells you parts of her story but offers you hope for your own."

— Annie Gebel, Tarot and Reiki Services, Trades of Hope

"What can I say about Tiiu Napp? She is an amazing woman. She is kind, caring, motivational, inspirational, and oh, so smart. The wisdom she shares with you is honest and from the heart. Tiiu is a great person to know professionally and personally. I'm so glad, proud, and lucky to have her in my life. She makes it that much better."

— Valarie Harris, Founder & President, Varris Marketing

"Tiiu Napp and I met a little more than five years ago. I have personally seen her grow from a timid, very insecure, self-conscious woman to a motivated, outgoing, and confident business owner and now author."

— Angel Mock, Le-Vel Top Leader + LV Millionaire Recipient, North Richland Hills, TX

"Tiiu Napp has written a book that is life transforming. She shares her trials as well as her victories in her personal quest to find true freedom. With an act of amazing courage, she openly shares in detail her struggles in her own life, and how she overcame them as she turned tragedy into victory! This book will transform your mind as well as your heart. Simply amazing!"

— Frank Reed, Author, Speaker, Coach, and CEO of Bottomline Ministries

"Tiiu Napp is someone who inspires her friends to grow beyond the limitations they've set for themselves. Through her own healing story, she shows us all how to conquer our fears while chasing after our dreams. If there are two words to describe her, they would be 'just love' because that's what she is to everyone and has for everyone she meets."

— Nickie Gullahorn, Sharla & Nickie Gullahorn, Le-Vel Top Leaders + LV Millionaire Recipients, Fort Worth, TX

"I had the pleasure of photographing Tiiu Napp for her book release. Her eyes truly are the windows to her soul and every image captured showed a life full of pain, strength, growth, and love. I've known Tiiu for several years now and her transformation has been incredible and a true inspiration for those around her. Her personality is infectious, and you can't walk away from a conversation with her without learning something about yourself as well. Her heart is exploding with love for others as she acknowledges them on their own paths of growth while gently nudging us to want to do better and be better. She's an amazing woman with much to share with the rest of us!"

— Debbie Gilman, Debbie Gilman Photography

"Tiiu Napp is a powerful person, using optimism and sheer will to experience life to the fullest. Her book, like her, is down to earth, yet rattles you. Then settles you with its positive and loving messages."

— Ryan M. Oliver, Author of the *Beasts of Men and Gods* Series

"In this incredible book, Tiiu Napp bares her soul to reveal to readers how she healed the holes in her soul. Her story of family dysfunction, some poor choices, and the courage to change and grow will leave you inspired to feel gratitude for all the good you have and motivated to change the areas of your life that still need work. I thank Tiiu for her brave, heartfelt writing of her story, and I know it will help countless others."

— Tyler R. Tichelaar, PhD and Award-Winning Author of *Narrow Lives* and *The Best Place*

"No one ever said creating your own destiny was easy. In *Healing the Holes in Your Soul*, Tiiu Napp reveals how her life got off track, and then how she took ahold of its reins to recreate her destiny, based on learning how to trust the right people and how to forgive and understand the wrong people. This book is a tour-de-force about human relationships, the deep longings we all need satisfied, and how to satisfy them."

— Patrick Snow, Publishing Coach and International Best-Selling Author of *Creating Your Own Destiny* and *Boy Entrepreneur*

"This is a heroic story of a journey that Tiiu embarked upon, unbeknownst to her, which was more harrowing and frightful than she could have ever imagined. She learned about the love and protection a mother has for her children. Her life story is filled with genuine life and death situations teaching her to survive and persevere. In the end, she found her self-worth, self-love, and self-esteem. Once you have read this book, you realize that Tiiu is a role model for all persons seeking a path to find their way. Her story inspires us to follow her path to freedom."

— Dr. Michael Gross, Transformational Coach, Spiritual Coach, International Best-Selling Author of *The Spiritual Primer*, and Founder of the Non-Profit Corporation
The International Institute of Self-Empowerment

Healing
the Holes in
Your Soul

Your Journey to Freedom
Begins Within

TIIU NAPP

FOREWORD BY DR. MICHAEL GROSS

AVIVA
PUBLISHING
New York

HEALING THE HOLES IN YOUR SOUL
Your Journey to Freedom Begins Within

Copyright © 2021 by Tiiu Napp. All rights reserved.

Published by:
Aviva Publishing
Lake Placid, NY
(518) 523-1320
www.AvivaPubs.com

While this book is based on true events, names of individuals have been changed to protect their privacy.

Address all inquiries to:
Tiiu Napp
480-223-7921
tiiunapp3@gmail.com
www.HealingTheHolesInYourSoul.com

ISBN: 978-1-63618-072-4
Library of Congress Control Number: 2021906002

Editors: Tyler Tichelaar and Larry Alexander, Superior Book Productions
Cover & Interior Layout Design: Fusion Creative Works
Author Photo: Debbie Gilman, Debbie Gilman Photography

Every attempt has been made to source properly all quotes.

Printed in the United States of America

First Edition

2 4 6 8 10 12

To My Forever Love, Ken

I came to you weary, carrying tattered pieces of my wounded soul.
I talked of darkness, emptiness, and feeling lonely.
No sense of purpose anymore.
I talked of hopes and dreams hidden in the memory of my childhood.
I chattered incessantly and lived chaotically,
searching for peace but moving too fast to see it.
In my turmoil, knowing your own grief, you took me in.
You nurtured me and showed me serenity.
Your voice gave me peace.
Your arms gave me comfort.
Your eyes showed me compassion and
your heart gave me love.
For all that you do, I am eternally grateful.
Through time you continue to teach, by your simple pleasures in life.
Today, I awoke to feel the warmth of sunshine embracing my happy heart.
I celebrate life and enjoy each day,
because you have renewed my heartfelt hopes and dreams.
I have found what I've been searching for.
My life is complete as long as you share each day with me.

— Always, Your Lady

Dedication

To my compassionate, loving mother, and my confident, creative father, who dance together in the Gardens of Heaven, my heart fills with gratitude for you both. You continue to inspire me with your wisdom and unconditional love. Your life from Estonia, through Sweden, and to Canada was challenging, yet your tenacity and courage continued to grow strong with the power of your love. The core values you taught me kept me alive, and I continue to honor them today.

There are two incredible men I must acknowledge first because they saved my life. My eternal gratitude that my prayers were answered when they entered my life. First, my best friend and lifetime companion, Ken McKean. When I was homeless and on the verge of giving up, Ken gave me hope, opened his home to me, and taught me to love and trust again. He saved my life and his children welcomed me into their family.

I thought my life was complete, but as time passed, I realized I was still searching for something. As my elders began to pass away, I yearned to find the one thing still missing in my life. When I met Dr. Michael Gross, author of *The Spiritual Primer*, I realized he holds the missing piece for all of us. He awakened my soul. Many of his quotes grace the pages of my book. Dr. Gross is humble and shares that he is a conduit for God, the True Source. To acknowledge and respect his work, you will see T. S. after his name. Today, I understand that everything we need to live our perfect life is within us. Both men continue to mentor me and encourage me to write my story and share it with the world.

With heartfelt gratitude and love, I must also acknowledge my children. My daughter has always been my pride and joy. My son is my rock and keeps me anchored with his humor and love. With respect to their privacy, I will not write names, but they, too, saved my life as you will read in the stories.

Life is fragile, and I have witnessed the passing of my parents and elders. I honor them as I share my heritage and will always cherish their unconditional love. They taught me many of the core values I continue to follow today.

I am honored to share my story with you, the reader. May my stories liberate you from your burdens in life and bring you new hope for a life of abundance.

Acknowledgments

My heart holds the deepest gratitude to Dr. Michael Gross. He is worthy of my sincere dedication and I must also acknowledge his incredible impact on my life. As we began working together on my spiritual growth, we became trusted friends. This book has been created because of his encouragement and mentorship. Michael has shown me the value of sharing my story and how it will help others who struggle with low self-esteem, low self-love, and low self-worth. Knowing that Michael accompanies me on this healing journey is truly a blessing. Healing and flourishing is a lifelong process.

I am grateful that Patrick Snow agreed to be my book coach. He has led me through the minutia of the book industry with skill, wisdom, and compassion. Patrick encouraged me to contact Dr. Michael Gross, Today, we have become a multi-dimensional family. I am honored to have Patrick as my leader in the industry.

To my good friend, Mary West, I give my most sincere gratitude. She has encouraged me to step out of my comfort zone many times. Mary introduced me to Patrick, who instilled this thought into my soul. There are only two things we leave in this world: our children and our art.

It is with great pride that I have been honored to have Tyler Tichelaar and Larry Alexander edit my manuscript. They have done an exceptional job in assembling the jigsaw puzzle of my stories.

To Rachel Langaker and Jessi Carpenter, thank you for the beautiful cover design and book layout. You have worked with me so diligently to create a powerful presentation of my bittersweet story.

Contents

"The best and most beautiful things in the world
cannot be seen or even touched.
They must be felt with the heart."

— Helen Keller

Foreword

Dr. Michael Gross

"Are you a servant of your fears, or the master of your life?"

— Dr. Michael Gross, T. S.

Healing the Holes in Your Soul by Tiiu Napp is the inspiring story of a young woman of great strength and fortitude who decided to walk out into the "wilderness" and explore life.

Warning: This book may change your life and empower you to heal your body, mind, soul, and spirit as Tiiu has. There are two paths one can take in life; the first is through logical understanding and explanation; the second is through life experiences. Tiiu chose the life-altering experiences to enhance her life so that, unbeknownst to her at that time, she can now share her story of inspiration with all of us. What is it that makes a person find the strength to endure the physical, mental, and emotional challenges in their life? Once you have read this book, you will understand how Tiiu's journey completed the greatest challenges in her life to become whole again.

At the time of this writing, I have known Tiiu for a little over fourteen months. When I first met her, she told me her book coach,

Patrick Snow, had recommended that we meet and talk about her life. We had a great discussion and she disclosed a little bit of information. Thereafter, she chose to hire me as her transformational coach. It has turned out to be one of the most exciting and positive experiences of my life. She told me she was going to be writing a book, yet at that time unnamed. In all my years as a transformational coach, my clients have shared many painful experiences with me. Those experiences helped form their lives up to the time I met them.

The experiences Tiiu shared with me tell of an incredible woman with great perseverance and strength to overcome the obstacles in her life to protect her children. Those life-altering experiences created a journey in which Tiiu miraculously found the inner strength to heal and find herself worthy of living. She was and is a very adventurous person who through her experiences began to appreciate life and realize her challenges opened the door to discovering her mission and goal in life.

Along the way, Tiiu muddled through life. She now knows it was a guiding force, and that force, known as God, the True Source, that protected and looked out for her. Tiiu discovered it was her mission and goal to arrive at this point in her life to be an inspiration to change the lives of abused women, men, and children.

I often reflect on what Tiiu has shared with me, which you will read in her book. She had amazing strength and tunnel vision to protect her children and survive at all costs. Many women, men, and children do not have the strength to persevere that Tiiu has.

The story starts when Tiiu is a young rebellious girl beginning a journey to experience life. As you will read, little did she know the types of experiences she would endure. An ordinary person would have caved in and ended their life, or been in a mental institution, or subjected themselves to cruel physical, mental, and emotional abuse. As you experience Tiiu's journey through her words, you can only realize how painfully uncomfortable it must've been at times, and yet what a great role model she is for all of us. Tiiu is a remarkable woman who realized through her inner spiritual journey that she is the sole director of her life. All the experiences she went through ended up empowering her. Tiiu understood, upon reflecting on those tumultuous experiences, that she needed to forgive herself and the perpetrators of them. Through this courageous powerful decision, she has evolved into the strong, compassionate, and loving woman she is today. Tiiu has demonstrated that where there is a will, there is a guiding inner force to overcome life's horrendous challenges. Where there is a guiding force, there is an inner guiding strength, and where there is an inner guiding strength, there is freedom to achieve your emancipation into self-empowerment. I do not state these words lightly because I firmly believe this force resides in all of us. Tiiu now knows that her guiding inner strength came from The True Source and she was never alone.

Tiiu has learned the way to find her real self, and consequently, she has become an inspiration for all of us to overcome our obstacles. At the tender age of sixty-seven, she received her black belt in Taekwondo. She has demonstrated her will and desire to face any obstacle with complete confidence, always knowing she will always end up a success in all her endeavors. In her forties, she challenged herself to successfully skydive as well as pursue other achievements. What is it in a person who goes through the trials and tribulations of life that makes them say, "I will work my way through this" and

"I am a survivor"? Tiiu told me many times that she felt she had no other choice but to work through her painful experiences so she could come out of a world that left her broken into a world of healing and love. Tiiu's motivating force was the love and protection of her children. Most people would stay stuck in their life of fear and continually be the victim, but not Tiiu. This is Tiiu's story as a survivor! It is a story of fortitude, success, and healing while leaving all the "scars" of life behind. It is about living in the moment.

As I further observed Tiiu, I realized that no matter how many times she fell, she picked herself figuratively and literally up off the floor, not knowing consciously what direction to take. Tiiu understood, somehow, that she was being guided by her soul to do the right thing for her family. She has demonstrated the leap of faith. With all of the trials, tribulations, and obstacles she faced, she kept walking the straight line to self-empowerment without ever realizing it. Only when Tiiu and I began to work together did she realize what a courageous person she is and what she has accomplished in this lifetime.

When Tiiu speaks, she speaks from the heart with great compassion and understanding. She is able to relate to all those who have gone through physical, emotional, and mental abuses because she has lived, experienced, and survived the same. We can learn much from Tiiu by realizing that with each challenge in a person's life, there is always inner strength to move on to the next step and onto the next step, until finally they find themselves free of their bondage of fear. Tiiu's incredible insight and understanding of life have now placed her in a position to help others—those frightened souls still stuck in a life of abuse and fear. Tiiu illuminates the path to follow to come out of the darkness into the light. Her experiences, her words of wisdom, and her life now have become a role model for all of humanity to read, embrace, live, and admire! She illustrates the way in her powerful book, *Healing the Holes in Your Soul.*

Respectfully,
Dr. Michael Gross

International Best-Selling Author of *The Spiritual Primer*
Founder of the Non-Profit Corporation *The International Institute of Self-Empowerment*
www.DrMichaelGross.com

Preface

Do You Hear Your Inner Voice?

"Listen to that still small voice within,
for in it you will find your answers."

— Anonymous

What guides your decisions? Life is a journey through a myriad of choices. The choices you make create the path to our destiny. Sometimes, it can be a very lonely journey, seldom peppered with joy and laughter. Other times, you may embrace the overwhelming sensation of love and gratitude. It is important to remember that everyone can see your outside, your body, and how you present yourself. Are you confident and positive, or are you timid and afraid? You, like everyone else, are always being judged. But no one can see your true core feelings unless you decide to share them. Those emotions are uniquely yours, and you have free will to share them or lock them deeply into the core of your soul. When you find yourself alone in your environment and alone in your thoughts, remember to look inside yourself. The answers you are seeking are right there inside you. You are not alone!

Stop the chaos in your mind. The cacophony of noises and voices are only a distraction and not what you are seeking. When the endless self-doubt, ego, and negativity reach a crescendo, remember you always have a choice. Be your own best friend and reach deep into your soul for the answers. Love, peace, and harmony are there just waiting for your trust. Unlock that door! You will be so grateful you did. Will you stand strong and honor your decisions?

You will learn in reading this book how influential Dr. Michael Gross has been in my life. He has transformed my life from fear, pain, and anxiety to a life of love, peace, joy, and freedom.

Therefore, with his permission, I purposely used many of Dr. Michael Gross's teachings and quotations throughout this book. It is my hope that his message of peace, healing, and unconditional love will have the same positive impact on your life that it has had on mine.

Introduction

Finding Your Purpose

"We can't control our destiny, but we can control who we become."

— Anne Frank

Survival is an endless raging river of choices. Imagine being faced with a decision while staring down the barrel of a loaded gun. Seconds tick away before you see the trigger finger begin to move. Perhaps no gun is pointing in your face, but you are hiding your toddler under blankets in a dark closet. Protecting your little child is your only thought as you hear yelling and angry pounding on the barricaded bedroom door. Do you know what it feels like to lock yourself in a bathroom, sitting with your back against the door, holding your children, and keeping them quiet, while their father is destroying the next room? When going face to face with your enemies, you must make split-second decisions. Sometimes you are dealing with strangers, but other times you may face the anger and rage of someone you love. An intense energy brings forth a hatred when a loving family member steps into a fury and lashes out. Panic leads to survival behavior, which determines how you will make your choices. Whether you experience an assault from a stranger or domestic violence, your decision at those most critical moments can alter the rest of your life.

In *Healing the Holes in Your Soul*, watch for the six main types of abuse: physical, sexual, verbal/emotional, mental/psychological, financial/economic, and cultural/identity. Then answer the focus questions, which are designed to make you aware of unhealthy behaviors and patterns that may lead to an escalating risk of domestic violence.

Focus Questions

1. Have you been ridiculed for your opinions? Briefly describe.

_____

_____

_____

2. Describe how you feel around a group of people, some of whom you don't know.

_____

_____

_____

3. If you were bullied as a child, describe what happened and how you felt.

_____

_____

_____

4. When you are speaking to someone, can you look them in the eye? What do you do when you can't?

_____

_____

_____

5. Were you harshly judged by your employer, your peers, or your
    family? If so, what did you do?

    _____

    _____

    _____

6. Have you caught yourself trying to prove your self-worth? Describe.

    _____

    _____

    _____

7. Do you struggle, living paycheck to paycheck, or having more
    month than money? What do you do to make it through the
    month?

    _____

    _____

    _____

8. Are you afraid to speak your mind? How do you cope?

    _____

    _____

    _____

If you have answered "yes" to any of these questions, you are not alone. Many individuals struggle with the same things. I have been right where you are now. Many times, I have had to choose between using my last few dollars to buy food or to buy gas so I could get to work. Many days, there was only enough food for my children.

Be kind to yourself as you begin to recognize that many of these difficulties and insecurities have woven themselves into your life through different relationships and situations. Life is a unique journey for each of us. Life is a mixture of rainbows and roses. But remember this…rainbows will fade, and even the most beautiful roses have thorns. Be cautious as you navigate life's rose gardens.

The book you are holding reflects my journey through some of my most painful moments. The stories aren't for the faint of heart, although they portray heartfelt moments. I have started many personal journals throughout the last five decades, and these writings encapsulate some of my most empowering moments. As I typed out some of the stories, tears rolled down my cheeks, but I was compelled to continue writing because I can no longer keep the experiences hidden within my secret memories. Many people struggle with similar events right now, as I write this introduction.

In this book, you will learn that survivors of abuse and domestic violence are an interesting breed. They are warriors. Like the lioness rearing her head to protect her young, they will sacrifice themselves in ways that would make the most courageous soldiers fall to their knees in tears. Abuse happens within every race, color, creed, and culture. There is no discrimination, only violence. Sadly, our children learn by watching us. They are like our mirror. In time, they become a direct reflection of what they see in us. As parents, we must ask ourselves, "What are we showing our children?"

When I was young, our family attended church every Sunday. I have always believed in God. But there are so many religions and different names for God, which, ultimately, lead us all to one True Source. For clarity I choose to follow Dr. Michael Gross' example and add "the True Source" after God. As a young adult, I was searching for the place where I fit. I attended many churches and researched many religions, but sadly, none of them completely resonated with me, so I continued searching for many years. As life progressed and I struggled with non-believers and abuse, I began to slip away and stopped searching for my life's purpose. Survival became my only goal, and protecting my children was my priority.

Now, I am honored to share my story with you so you can witness the transformation that has taken me from tears of heartache to overwhelming tears of unconditional love. Within this book, you will read not only about my struggles but my victories! At times, things may resonate within you as you become inspired by my story. Think about how to recreate your own perfect life. Please remember, these are my experiences of what inspired me to make the choices I did. Everyone has a unique purpose, and it is my hope that as you follow my journey, you will discover your own purpose. It took me many decades to realize my purpose. Now, knowing that sharing my painful challenges and my journey of personal growth will help empower others, it is my goal to bring hope and unconditional love to those who continue to struggle.

Every life is a story continuously unfolding. Are you the author of your story, or is someone else using your pen and writing your destiny? Ask yourself, "Who is controlling my life?"

If you have been seeking a way out of abuse, or are gathering the courage to leave, or are wondering what to do now that you are in your brave new world, the stories, quotes, and focus questions written in these pages will help you find your answers. My hope is that as you read this book, you will draw from it inspiration and courage to move toward your greatest potential. We all have a story to tell; may your future be filled with abundance, joy, happiness, and unconditional love. As you reconnect with your soul and step into the beautiful person you truly have within you, you will experience a new level of self-worth, self-love, and self-esteem.

I wish you much joy, growth, and success in your journey. Let's begin!

Prelude

Emotion Is an Energy

"It is love alone that leads to right action.
What brings order in the world is to love and let love do what it will."

— Jiddu Krishnamuri

What is emotion? It seems like a simple question, until we begin to define the essence of emotion's source. The book you hold in your hand is my personal journey, through the swill beneath the gutter of life. This sounds like a dark journey, and yes, at times it is. But sprinkled in the sadness are moments of overwhelming joy and intense love.

As you read the stories, you will be taken through some of my greatest challenges. I will show how survival and protecting our children are our natural instincts and how love is the glue that holds our lives together. Included among my life stories, you will read about some of the people who inspired me. I will share how their stories gave me hope to keep moving through each painful moment and embrace the tender moments of love. These inspiring stories show how many of us have called upon our inner warriors to stare down the demons of fear.

One thing that has become evident to me while writing this book is the common thread among the women who have inspired me: Helen Keller, Anne Frank, Amelia Earhart, Princess Diana, and my grandmother—we called her Mutti. These individuals are a diverse group; however, each one was tempered with tenacity and integrity. No matter what people were saying or what was going on around them, each one continued to live by right action and correct exchange. I am grateful I have learned about these individuals because they continually inspired me while I was struggling to hold onto a tiny fiber of hope.

When we are denied our primal urge to cry out during intense fear, pain, heartache, or passion, we lose a piece of our soul. It fragments into our core as we feel it slip away. We may do an excellent job covering it up, but do we really? Through challenging years, more and more of our soul fragments and we come to feel lost and alone. We continue with our life, our jobs, raising our families, and the chaotic demands of adulthood. Our focus is constantly being redirected away from nurturing our soul. Our focus is purely on survival!

Challenging moments create triggers that may lie dormant within us for years. Those wounds are buried so deeply within our core that we need to recognize them to begin the healing process. If we ignore the wounds, they will continue to fester and eat away at our soul, like a parasite. That negative energy will destroy our body's cellular structure. Disease will be created in the body and the quality of our life will shrink into one of mediocrity. Just one word, one smell, one touch, one thought, one action from another person, perhaps a loved one, and suddenly, the hair on the back of the neck stands up. The body becomes tense, and every fiber of our being is rigid and on high alert. Defense mode! What are your triggers? Will you take flight, stay to fight, or freeze?

Survivors of abuse and domestic violence are an interesting breed. They are survivors—they are warriors, like lionesses rearing their heads to protect their young. Women and men continue to survive atrocities in silence, staying in toxic and often life-threatening relationships. They will die for the safety of their children. In certain ethnic cultures, young women will be caught in arranged marriages and suffer abuse silently to honor family code.

According to the National Coalition Against Domestic Violence (NCADV), in the United States, more than 10 million adults experience domestic violence annually. If an individual living in the United States experienced only one incident of violence in their lifetime, that would equate to one episode of violence every three seconds. However, in many cases, individuals endure repeated abuse. This information was retrieved from a 2018 report. At that time, statistics for domestic violence had increased 20 percent from 2016 totals. Statistics are still being gathered for the increase in domestic violence since the Covid-19 pandemic began in early 2020. The numbers have increased because more people are remaining home, often with their abusers.

Abuse has many faces, and often, women are not the only victims. Unfortunately, intimate partner violence (IPV) of both genders also fall victim to domestic violence and the myriad faces of abuse. Awareness and speaking out about abuse are paramount for breaking the cycle of violence.

When I was caught up in the fear of abuse and physical violence, I felt I had no voice. Limited resources for help were available in my community. The local police were few and far between, and they were often unable to provide any assistance. A cloak of negativity covered any victim who reported abuse. Abuse was thought to be a fallacy, and victims were considered in need of psychological help. Many times, I thought I was losing my mind and wondered what body part I would have to cut off to throw at local officers to get their attention.

As you read my story, remember that everything in life is an energy. At times, my energy was totally depleted! When I felt I had nothing left inside me, I just wanted to curl up and die. But I knew a driving force was within me that gave me the courage to pick myself up, dust myself off, and give life one more chance. My grandmother, Mutti, was my inspiration. I share her story to honor her in this book.

Today, I know we always have free will to choose. No matter how long we have been trapped in a fear-based mindset, we can choose to change our destiny. Will you choose negativity cloaked in fear, or positivity surrounded in love? Only you know what choice you will make. Are you ready to unwrap the greatest gift of your life...love? Your journey begins by loving yourself!

Part I

The Early Years

Chapter 1

Introduction to My Heritage

Honor

"In many ways, each of us is the sum total
of what our ancestors were.
The virtues they had may be our virtues,
their strengths our strengths, and,
in a way, their challenges
could be our challenges."

— James E. Faust

For you to truly grasp the experiences I am about to share, it is important for you to know something about my heritage. My parents were raised under old school rules. The rules were strict and enforced with an iron hand. My sisters and I were raised under the same strict rules; however, times were changing in the 1950s and 1960s. Our family needed to adapt to different lifestyles in two different countries. Estonia was under Soviet Rule and our family was adjusting to life in Canada. I struggled with the strict rules while watching my friends experience afterschool activities and going to movies unsupervised. I often wondered why my parents were so strict while my friends appeared to be living without strict rules. Today, I admire my parents for the values they instilled in us as young children. Those values are what I drew upon when my life was difficult.

My family is deeply rooted in the small Baltic country of Estonia. Officially, it is the Republic of Estonia, and it is located on the eastern coast of the Baltic Sea in Northern Europe. Simply stated, this small, unique country is south of Finland and east of Sweden.

During the Middle Ages, Estonia was ruled by Denmark, the German Knights of the Livonian Order, and Sweden. From the eighteenth century until the early twentieth century, Estonia was part of the Russian Empire. As a young adult, my paternal grandfather was part of the Czarist Russian Army. My father once told me that when he was a young boy, he saw my grandfather's military rifle hanging on the wall in my grandfather's blacksmith shop. My grandfather caught him admiring the rifle and sternly warned him never to touch it.

My father was born in 1924 on the family farm on the island of Hiiumaa, and my mother was born in 1929 in the capital city of Tallinn. Estonia is steeped in rich history that goes back to the twelfth century. Researching our genealogy, I realized some of our family traits can be traced back to the Vikings. Archaeological discoveries include a unique find of 100 Viking-age swords that appear to date from the middle part of the tenth century. Ian Harvey's article "Huge Hoard of 100 Viking Swords Found in Estonia" was published in the *Vintage News* on October 12, 2019. Harvey writes that between 800 and 1200 CE, Viking warriors were known to raid areas within what is now known as Estonia, as well as Greenland, and as far away as Newfoundland, Canada.

This information makes my ancestry research more valid. Since my parents are full-blooded Estonians, my ancestors have lived around the Baltic Sea for many generations. As you read these chapters, you will discover the core values that have driven me through years of turmoil and self-sabotage. These values stem from the "Viking Honor System," which has since been relabeled the "Nine Noble Virtues," and are similar to the Knight's Code of Chivalry. I recognized that many of my father's traits align with these Nine Noble Virtues:

1. Courage
2. Truth/Honesty
3. Honor
4. Fidelity/Loyalty
5. Discipline
6. Hospitality
7. Industriousness
8. Self-Reliance
9. Perseverance/Tenacity

I have learned that as we conquer our challenges, we empower ourselves. That self-empowerment begins our journey to freedom. I merged the following moral codes to the Viking Honor System. Together, the Nine Noble Virtues and my six moral codes are the foundation of the "15 Steps to Your Freedom." You will find them as chapter topics. The six I added are:

1. Love
2. Integrity
3. Trust
4. Forgiveness/Gratitude
5. Resilience
6. Curiosity

In retrospect, I have recognized that my father, Arno (not his real name), took great pride in his heritage. (To protect my family's privacy, I will use fake names for my parents, relatives, and other people mentioned in this book.) My father honored his Fatherland with his last breath. He knew it would only be a matter of time before he would be expected to serve in either the Nazi or Red Army. He has an incredible story on how he joined a few local young men as they planned their departure to Sweden. With Soviet occupation imminent, many Estonians were leaving their homeland.

During the bombings in Tallinn, in 1944, my maternal grandmother, Mutti, was taking her daughters to Germany. Mutti had a friend in Mittenwald who offered them shelter. My fourteen-year-old mother, Nora, and seven-year-old sister, Ella, would have an opportunity to finish school. It would be a few years before they relocated to Sweden. Details of this part of their story are vague. We don't know what happened to Nora and Ella's father during 1944-1946.

Many Estonian refugees, once processed in Sweden, were given jobs in textile factories. My mother told me she was assigned to make lace in a textile factory near Gingri. My father worked on the looms and drove delivery trucks.

My parents met at a local dance in Fristad and realized they both worked at the same factory. They seldom shared stories about this time in their life. Perhaps it was from fear someone would report to the Russians where they had gone. Due to the Soviet occupation of Estonia during World War II, many immigrants who had left the country were fearful they would be found by Soviet spies. They protected their freedom by not sharing their past with people. They only spoke more openly to fellow Estonians who had also left their homeland. My parents were together more than sixty years. Truly a loving couple, they spent many years dancing together and building a good life in Canada.

It has always been my goal to share my family heritage with my children. During the early years after the end of Soviet Occupation in Estonia, I was honored to travel to the land of my roots and finally hear the family stories of escape and the stories of those who never left the homeland. You will find some of the family history woven through the pages of this book. But I need to return to addressing the "15 Steps to Your Freedom."

Honor and Love go hand in hand when it comes to family relationships. Sadly, time moves quickly as we struggle to build good lives for our families. We are often so focused on providing the basic needs that there is little time to build relationships. Knowing what my family endured during the years after the war, I watched and learned about the virtues, but the one thing lacking was a nurturing relationship with my parents. I must add that my parents always provided a good home and food and all our physical needs were met, but there was little time for nurturing relationships. After my first few trips to Estonia, my parents and I began building a new understanding of each other. Sadly, time with my aging parents would be limited.

I remember the day as if it were yesterday when I promised my mother right before she passed away that I would call dad every day and visit him once a month until he no longer needed me. He continued to live in the house he built in Victoria, British Columbia, for several years after the passing of my mother. I was living a short distance away in the USA. Travel, including the ferry ride from Port

Angeles, Washington, to Victoria was a 3-4 hour trip. I made a point of always spending time with my father.

We spent our time together talking about my father's life on the farm and how World War II changed so many things for his family. We also spent hours talking about faith, family, life after death, and whether there was life on other planets, perhaps in other galaxies. Yes, we even talked about aliens and Area 51. During these times, I saw the man my mother fell in love with. He was proud, strong, and courageous, but also romantic, gentle, and loving. We shared the same sense of humor, and we often had the staff at the nursing home smiling and joining in our jokes.

In 2015, at the age of ninety-one, my father could no longer care for himself. He sold the home I had grown up in and moved into a nursing home. We often sat on the edge of his bed in the elder care home as he told me stories of his life during World War II and how he met my mother in Sweden. As I listened, I began to understand his love for his homeland, his courage and need to protect his family, and how important it was to him to always be honorable. Yes, his strict disciplinary tactics were challenging for me growing up. At times, I struggled to understand why it was so hard for my parents to adapt to a life in Canada. Today, I have the utmost respect for my parents because they leave a powerful legacy.

It took years for me to understand their mindset. When I traveled to Estonia to visit family and friends, I finally began to understand how much my father valued his heritage and why. In the last few years of his life, my father wrote his autobiography. Sadly, his life ended before I read his story—my life was so busy that I did not take the time to read it while he was alive. Today, I regret the time wasted not reading his autobiography. I have so many unanswered questions. As I spent time with my father in the nursing home, in the last few years of his life, I was finally able to become his true friend. He no longer treated me like a child who needed guidance. He respected me as an adult with my own opinions. We finally created a nurturing relationship.

Many things baffled me growing up because when I asked my parents questions about their lives in the war, they refused to answer. They indicated that children did not need to know the stories. Those things were revealed to me, much later, during our father-daughter talks. My father told me that thousands of Estonians had fled their homeland during World War II. Many were found by the Russians and returned to Estonia to be disciplined. Word got out that many never made it back to their Estonian homes. My uncle was one who never returned. We have heard rumors about what happened to him, but we believe he became sick and passed away in a camp in Siberia. Letters that were mailed into Estonia to family and friends were monitored, and many letters never arrived at all.

I would like to share with you a story my father told me about his life during this time.

My father began his story when he was in Sweden working on a Russian road crew. He recalled walking to town with a few friends and spotting a young woman carrying a basket of flowers. A flower fell out of her basket and one of my dad's friends called out, "Someone pick it up. It will bring you luck." My father grabbed it and tucked it into his pocket.

As a young girl, looking at my father's photo album from his time in Sweden, I found the flower my father had picked up that day, dried and wrapped in cellophane, complete with Estonian flag-colored ribbons, and taped onto the inside of the hand-painted front cover of the photo album.

This event happened during World War II. As a young Estonian man, my father had to decide if he would join the Red Army (Russia) or the Estonian division of the Waffen-SS (German Nazi Party). Dad disliked both military forces because they were bombing his homeland. But knowing he had to choose, or the government would choose for him, he chose the Waffen-SS—only because it had an Estonian division. He was given documents and a date to report for duty in Tallinn.

My father was already planning his next move, just as if he were playing a game of chess. He doctored the report date (with a poor ink match) and headed back to Hiiumaa. His goal was to get back to his family without being captured.

Living on an island comes with challenges. At a very volatile time for everyone, someone saw Dad on a ferry going back to Hiiumaa and reported him to the Germans. When he did not report as ordered, the SS sent men to find my father. Dad had worked at the regional district office in Koorgesaare next to the post office. When he returned to the island, he stopped in to visit his friend Edgar and arranged for Edgar to warn him when the SS was coming. Edgar would cut across the fields on his bicycle to warn Dad. My dad and his father had built a couple of false walls into their house at Nabi Talu so they had a place Dad could hide.

When the SS showed up at the post office looking for my father, Edgar sent them to the neighbors' house and rode off to warn my dad.

For some reason, the family dog did not bark when the SS showed up, so my father did not have time to hide beneath the trap door under the bed. He squeezed inside the false wall beside the kitchen table. As the soldiers approached the house, my grandmother politely greeted them. She said she had no idea where Arno was. She showed the officers the last letter he had written home, which was postmarked in Poland. Then she invited the SS soldiers into the house for sandwiches and vodka. They accepted and enjoyed the feast served by my grandmother—all the while, my father listened to the conversation from the other side of the wall. The SS finally left. My father knew he would have to go into hiding elsewhere on the island until he could find a way to safety in Sweden.

In June of 1997, I spent some time with family on the island of Hiiumaa. My father had built a small house on the farmland, and he shared many stories of growing up, caring for livestock and his garden. I vividly remember the day I watched my elderly father standing on the rocks on the beach at Kootsaare Otsast gazing across the Baltic Sea toward the rocky coastline of Sweden. As the waves danced across the sandy, rocky beach, the sun was beginning to set, and the air became chilly as he fastened his jacket and pulled up his collar. He was deep in thought and sighed as he began to speak, softly sharing his story…. This would be the last time my father would stand on this hallowed spot, looking out across the Baltic Sea.

I watched his expressions while he was remembering the feelings of that historic day. Wisps of his gray hair blew out from under his hat. His voice became softer as he pointed to a large rock in the water that had been a marker during his story. It was early May in 1944. After months of hiding from the Red Army and Nazis, he met up with a few other young men, some old school friends. They were all in the same situation and working to prepare a boat they would navigate across the rough waters of the Baltic to Sweden and freedom.

On the first attempt at the crossing, the boat ran into many problems. The crew returned to shore and postponed the trip due to a bad storm and a problem with the motor. It was a bad combination, and the boat had no speed. A better mast, sail, and stronger engine were needed for the difficult journey. They also needed to restock their food and water.

When the preparations were complete, Arno put his important papers in a waterproof packet in his pocket. He wore extra clothing. He hugged his mother and sisters as he bid them farewell. When he said goodbye to his father, my grandfather gave him a small compass. He said, "Safe journey, my son. This will help guide you."

On May 10, 1944, at approximately 10:00 p.m., under the cover of darkness, my father joined five other young men escaping Estonia. They left from Kootsaare Otsast, glancing back briefly for a final look at their homeland. The big rock he mentioned to me was the last sign of home as they began their voyage. Six brave young men navigated a twenty-two-foot boat powered by a little three-horsepower motor and nine-foot sail across the Baltic. Large ships have succumbed to the power of the water of the Baltic Sea. The idea of navigating a small vessel for twenty-three hours across rough waters and jagged rock outcroppings was very dangerous. However, the brave young men stayed strong to their mission.

The journey was difficult. The crossing was very rough due to snowstorms on the water. As the boat bounced around in the Baltic Sea, the onboard compass fell overboard. Navigating by the stars was virtually impossible due to heavy clouds. Arno reached into his pocket and pulled out the small compass his father had given him. Twenty-three hours later, the wet and weary young men made landfall in Swedish Skarguntens. Cold, wet, and weary, they were rescued by Swedish military and transported to an outpost called Norrtalje.

They were fed and given dry clothes, and my father was given a heavy, weatherproof coat that he would use for years. Decades later, I found this incredible piece of history hanging on a nail in the garage of his Victoria home.

The young men were housed courtesy of the Stockholm Ministry of Refugees at a camp in Vikingshill. Once released from the refugee camp, the six young men parted ways. Dad worked at Tynningd Camp on an emergency road construction crew in Blekinge County in the south of Sweden.

When my father told me this story on the beach that day, it had been more than fifty years since he had left his homeland on that dark night in May 1944. I share this story because my father instilled his moral core values deeply into my soul. It was my honor to have stood with him on that shore as he shared his story.

When I was a young girl in school, teachers asked me what my father did during the war. I created a story about him working with the French Resistance. It was a young girl's imagination because I could not understand why he had kept things from us. I understand now that he was protecting us. But as a child, I thought if Dad were a member of the French Resistance, I could justify not knowing more information.

Focus Questions

1. What is your first childhood memory?

_____

_____

_____

_____

_____

_____

2. Were you a curious adventure seeker? Describe an adventure.

_____

_____

_____

_____

_____

_____

3. Explain how you were disciplined.

_____

_____

_____

_____

_____

_____

4. What values and moral codes did your parents teach you?

_____

_____

_____

_____

_____

_____

5. How have you instilled those moral codes into your children?

_____

_____

_____

_____

_____

_____

6. How did you achieve your goal? If you didn't, what stopped you?

_____

_____

_____

_____

_____

_____

Summary

The term "honor" brings forth a few definitions. But in general terms, it leads to respect and recognizing the quality of an individual. As you answer the questions, consider the emotions you felt when the memories returned. As children, our thinking is molded in many ways. Those influences shape our thinking deep into our adult life. That's why it's important to recognize whether the memories are positive or negative. One thing to remember is that it is important to honor elders, but it is also important that you are respected as a unique individual. It is important to identify your personal value system.

Chapter 2

Choosing Freedom

Tenacity

"Our lives are fashioned by our choices. First, we make our choices. Then our choices make us."

— Anne Frank

North America is a melting pot of immigrants from a myriad of cultures; many of those immigrants came during World War II. My parents, grandparents, and three aunts were among the thousands of immigrants. My father and his family arrived in Montreal, Quebec in 1949. My mother arrived in Canada in 1950, followed in 1951 by her sister, her mother, and her mother's new husband. Many Estonians were settling in Eastern Canada and the USA. It was a time of settling into a new life in a new country and the birth of the Baby Boomer Generation.

In the early years, as our family was adapting to life in Canada, many Estonians remained guarded. The Soviets had occupied Estonia. The Estonians who had left their homeland were hearing from family left behind that letters and packages were being monitored during transit. The Soviets were making an effort to locate the people who left and bring them back to Estonia for disciplinary actions.

As I was growing up, knowing that my parents had endured traumatic relocation, I began reading *The Diary of Anne Frank.* My elders spoke little about their life and their escape from Estonia during World War II when the Germans and Russians were in conflict over possession of Estonia. Rightfully so, in some ways, my parents and both sets of grandparents were trying to remain private while living in Canada. They did not physically hide but kept limited correspondence with family and friends still living in Estonia. There was concern that if the Soviets found their friends communicating with an Estonian who had left the country, their friends would be in danger. With the passing of the last family elder, my father, I feel their story can now be shared.

Reading Anne Frank's story of life in the secret annex inspired me to understand more about the fears and adjustments my family experienced.

In June of 1942, the Nazis were working harder than ever to exterminate the Jewish population, a goal that became known as the Holocaust. In the summer of 1942, when Anne Frank's sister Margo was summoned to the Jewish Council of Amsterdam to report for "labor service" in a German-occupied territory, the Frank family went into hiding. The family knew what would happen if they were found. They had heard of many families that were taken away, night after night, in green and gray military vehicles.

During the same time, young men in Estonia were ordered to report for German or Russian military service. Many families were torn apart or taken as a family unit. Few returned to their farms. As mentioned earlier, my uncle perished in Siberia, but the details of his death are still unknown. Many brave young men who honored their country and freedom found a variety of ways to leave their homeland. Thousands of Jewish Estonians were also gathered and taken to labor or concentration camps.

As I continued to read Anne Frank's story, I realized how much courage and tenacity my own family showed. There was a powerful reason they maintained silence about their journey to Sweden, then to Canada. This was a time when people lived in fear of being discovered in their new homeland. With Soviet occupation in Estonia, the well-being of the family members and friends left behind was at risk. People were cautious about trusting others and worried about who might overhear their story of escape.

It would be years before my father told me he had built two hiding places in his father's farmhouse in Estonia. I found a pencil drawing in his old files that showed exactly where the false wall was and the hiding spot beneath the bed. Finding the drawing reminded me of the story my father once told me about the time German soldiers had come to the farmhouse looking for him because he didn't report for service. He was hiding in the false wall in the kitchen right beside the table. His mother was feeding the officers sandwiches and vodka. My father heard the entire conversation and was impressed by how cordial his mother acted.

Every family has a backstory; do you know yours? It has taken me many years to separate fact from fear because of our family legacy. But by knowing the past, I have a greater understanding of the stories being shared.

My mother, Nora, was born in Tallinn in 1929. A privileged child from an affluent family, she was sent to a private school. She was the oldest of two daughters, and often assigned to watch over her sister, who was seven years younger. The young family was living in a prominent apartment building owned by Nora's father in a popular business district.

During World War II, families were separated, and people often suffered lifelong trauma. When Tallinn was bombed, in 1944, fourteen-year-old Nora and her seven-year-old sister Ella were living with her father. Nora's parents had separated and the marriage was over. My maternal grandmother, Mutti, had separated from her husband and returned to the apartment to take her daughters away from the city during the heavy bombing throughout the city of Tallinn. The damage was so extensive that it was difficult to find landmarks in the rubble. Nora's father Eric remained in Tallinn at that time. This part of his story is unknown. However, he was found living in Sweden a few years later.

During the height of World War II, Mutti focused all her courage on keeping her daughters safe. I have heard a few stories, and I would like to share this one. Mutti was an inspiration to me in many ways. I admired her tenacity as she navigated her way to safety, while not having all the travel documents required for Nora. Mutti was ingenious in finding ways to keep her daughters safe in bomb shelters at night, while searching for food. Despite all the challenges, she found her way to her friend's home in Mittenwald, Germany, close to the Swiss border. The trio adapted to life in Germany, and the girls were able to continue school. Eventually, they relocated to Sweden as the war continued to escalate.

When my parents met in Sweden, young love blossomed. Sadly, the couple were torn apart three months after they met. Arno and his family had accepted contracts to work in a textile factory in Quebec, Canada. Farewells were bittersweet, but the young lovers wrote letters and kept the romance alive. The handwritten letters traveled back and forth across the Atlantic for more than a year. One letter contained a marriage proposal and a wedding ring. Today, I treasure their faded letters that traveled across the Atlantic Ocean.

After many months of planning and saving money, Nora finally secured a ticket on the *MS Gripsholm*, which took her from Gothenberg, Sweden, to Halifax, Ontario. The ship, built in 1924, was of great historical importance because it was the first ocean liner built for transatlantic express service as a diesel-powered vessel. My twenty-year-old mother traveled on her own; the rest of the family remained in Sweden until they were able to gather the money to travel to Canada. Many Estonians were traveling on the same vessel, but Nora didn't know them. She was very shy and later told me she stayed away from most people. She struggled with sea sickness during most of the long journey to Halifax. New immigrants were lined up in rows to be processed at Pier 21, much like the immigrants who would be going to Ellis Island in the USA. Once processed into Canada, she needed to find her way to the train station. Nora just needed to board a train to where Arno would meet her. She sent him a telegram with the train information and time of arrival at her destination. Unfortunately, Nora boarded the wrong train, and when Arno received the telegram, he sent a telegram to the train conductor instructing him to help Nora get off at a different stop. Saint-Hyacinthe, Quebec, would be her new stop. Had she remained on the train, she would have been taken to a center for refugees in Montreal, and Arno would have been unable to get her out for several weeks. Part of the agreement with the Canadian government was that Arno and Nora must get married within a specific timeframe. If she was in the camp in Montreal, she risked being returned to Sweden. Happily, the couple wed and spent more than sixty years together, which is a truly exceptional accomplishment.

My paternal grandparents and aunts relocated to Toronto after their contract at Dominion Textile ended in Sherbrooke, Quebec. My parents remained in Sherbrooke, where Arno worked an additional year after he completed his contract with the textile company. In 1952, after the birth of my older sister Helen, the young family relocated to Toronto and lived with my paternal grandparents. I was born in 1953, in the early years of the Baby-Boomer generation.

Many immigrants cautiously stayed in contact with others from their homeland. They worked to help other Estonians travel to Canada. I learned years later that my father helped my mother's father, Eric, immigrate to Canada. It is uncertain where Eric was during the time Mutti and her daughters were living in Sweden. Mutti had met a very kind and gentle man. We called him Isa. Mutti, Isa, and my aunt Ella had immigrated in March 1951 and were also living in Toronto. After talking to fellow Estonians, Mutti's curiosity was piqued when some of her Estonian friends heard there was plenty of work on the west coast of Canada. A few Estonians began traveling across Canada to Vancouver Island, British Columbia. It didn't take much time for Mutti, Isa, and my aunt Ella to embark on their way to settle in Victoria, British Columbia. I honestly believe I inherited my grandmother's nomadic soul.

As the family began settling into new lives, my father's side of the family stayed in Toronto. My older sister Helen had come down with colic when my parents realized my mother was pregnant. They really had not planned to have another baby. Unfortunately, I was often referred to as their little accident, but they always added that they loved me anyway. I had no idea those words would resonate with me the rest of my life. I was born in 1953 at Grace Hospital. My parents would hear beautiful things about life on the west coast of Canada. Mutti kept encouraging my parents to move west. Nora desperately wanted to be closer to her mother, and Arno had asthma and felt that working in construction would be better for his health. The construction industry was booming in Victoria, so he knew he could find work.

We began our move west in 1956. My first memory of Canada is of Niagara Falls, when my mother grabbed my pants to keep me from falling into the giant waterfall. Back then, we could stand extremely close to the edge. I was an incredibly curious child and probably quite a handful.

My paternal family members were once again separated because they stayed in Toronto, while my mother's side of the family went to the West Coast. At that time, the Trans-Canada Highway was under construction, and traveling across Canada was challenging. I barely remember the trip, but I do remember we slept in a tent we set up close to our 1950 Pontiac parked alongside the road. My father later told me it was a five-day drive because road conditions were poor, and he took a detour through the US.

As we drove through the Pacific Northwest, I remember my mother being in awe. She said it reminded her of the countryside in Estonia.

When my father drove the car onto the ferry, I remember how happy my parents felt to be beginning their new life on Vancouver Island. My father loved island life, and my mother was so excited to be living near her mother again. Our lives were enriched by so many blessings and family memories.

It took courage for my parents and grandparents to overcome their challenges and find a new life of freedom in Canada. They worked hard and studied the new language and lifestyle. It took time for them to adapt and raise their children in this new environment, but they did. Through their tenacity, resilience, and unconditional love, they led lives of honor, always respecting Estonian traditions.

As I read *The Diary of Anne Frank*, I realized that during the Nazi era in Germany, many families went into hiding throughout Europe like Anne Frank's family did. Estonian Jews were also being collected and loaded like cattle onto trains, so they tried to hide when they could. Sadly, only Otto Frank, Anne's father, survived to return to the secret annex. A loyal helper named Meip Gies salvaged Anne's diary and loose pages of notes after the family and other residents of the secret annex were taken in the Gestapo's raid on August 4, 1944. Everyone was arrested and removed to a Nazi concentration camp. They were hastily transported on the last train to Auschwitz. Meip returned Anne's written memories to her father. Later, a museum was created in the building where the secret annex is located. Today, Anne's diary is on display in a protective case in the room where the family spent 761 days in hiding.

As a teenager, I read Anne Frank's book several times, and as an adult, I visited the house in Amsterdam. It was an honor to climb the narrow, worn, wooden stairs hidden behind the bookcase. Walking through the secret annex brought the essence of life in hiding into my soul. There was little left of the furniture, but glued to the stained walls were small notes and pictures, the remnants of the spirit of a young teenager. It has been seventy-seven years since the family was taken by the Nazis and life in the secret annex ended.

The essence and spirit of a young girl named Anne continues to linger in the once secret annex.

Nora was close to the same age as Anne Frank when she was in hiding. Nora was not in hiding, but she shared her experience of being left alone on the roadside to watch baggage while several German soldiers were sitting close by. It happened when Mutti was taking them from Estonia to Germany. Seven-year-old Ella was terrified of the bombings and was hysterical. Mutti had to leave Nora on the roadside watching their suitcases while she carried her screaming seven-year-old daughter into the woods to calm her down. Nora sat gazing downward, afraid to look up and make eye contact with the soldiers.

Even with her gaze averted, Nora noticed the young German soldiers staring at her, talking, and joking. My mother was petrified that the soldiers would come toward her, but she heard one of them say, "She's too young; not even a woman for us to enjoy." When I was fourteen and my mother shared this story with me, she giggled a little when she added how grateful she was to have been a late-bloomer.

It is important to remember the choices our parents made were not always choices they wanted to make, but what they did molded us into the people we have become. Decisions made in the past cannot be changed, but we can always choose to change the person we have become, regardless of those influences. Anne Frank showed us that even trapped and hiding, the power of our mind and unconditional love will give us the strength to endure. There may be times when our physical bodies are trapped in prisons of ill health or abusive situations, but those who survive the atrocities are the ones who choose to free their minds.

Focus Questions

1. Write some highlights of your family's backstory.

_____

_____

_____

_____

_____

_____

2. How did your ancestors fight for freedom?

_____

_____

_____

_____

_____

3. Are your elders immigrants? If yes, explain.

_____

_____

_____

_____

_____

_____

4. What traits of courage and tenacity did they share with you?

_____

_____

_____

_____

_____

Summary

As we consider the values systems of our parents and grandparents, we need to consider the choices they made at difficult times. It is important to know how their lives were influenced as they emerged into adulthood. In sharing these stories, I could see the tenacious courage each family member had to endure the challenges of the unknown so they could live a life of freedom. By having a greater understanding of our family members' pasts, we discover a greater understanding of how and why we were influenced the way we were.

Chapter 3

Childhood Adventures

Curiosity/Love

"Within your heart, there lies an energy that is immutable
and contains the primordial essence
of the beginning of the universe called LOVE!"

— Dr. Michael Gross, T. S.

As the flow of life, created from unconditional love, begins within the womb, the unborn is learning and developing. It is our duty to honor that growing miracle, nurture it, and enrich the life within by sharing the power of love.

Research shows that the unborn can hear sounds within the mother's body and in the outer world. In the article "What Babies Learn in the Womb," Laura Flynn McCarthy writes that babies begin engaging many senses during the last trimester of pregnancy, and external and internal sounds stimulate reactions in the fetus. Studies show that unborn children are learning language, reacting to light, and developing a palate for discriminating tastes.

The fetus hears both internal and external sounds. Research has found a correlation between the mother's voice and the sounds and vibrations the child feels within the womb. Knowing this, and understanding that we are all an aspect of God, the True Source, is it incorrect to think an unborn child can also feel another's emotional energy?

Ideally, during pregnancy, the fetus develops in a healthy environment, but what happens if the surroundings are hostile or abusive? The negative energy around the pregnant woman can affect the fetus' development in many ways. The long-term effects on the child may not be revealed until long after birth.

Our children learn by watching us. They are like our mirror…in time, they will become a direct reflection of what they see in us. What reflection are you showing them? Take a moment to think about how you treat others. More importantly, how are you treating yourself?

As a young child, I often watched my mother get dressed up for a special evening with my father and their friends. She always hated her body, complained about her weight, wore a hairpiece, and never left the house without applying her lipstick. She always dropped her compact and lipstick container into her purse, and then took a tissue and pressed it between her lips. Many a time she gave me her tissue with the lipstick prints on it, and I would try to put a smudge of lipstick on my lips.

Remember your thoughts are things:

- Are your words positive or negative?
- Do you think before you speak?
- Do you think before you judge yourself?
- Are your children hearing you criticizing yourself?
- What are you manifesting?

What Makes You Unique?

I have often thought, *If we are products of the same two parents, why are Helen and Margaret and I so different?* Siblings may all learn from the same parents, but we may forget to realize that parents change and grow as their children grow. My sisters and I were all very different children, so the lessons we learned were contingent upon how we processed them. My older sister, Helen, shared qualities with my father. She was strong-willed, stubborn, and very independent. Dad never showed tears, not even when my mom died. He once told me that showing emotions, like sadness and love, was a sign of weakness. My younger sister Margaret was more like my mother. She was needy, lacked self-confidence, and wanted everyone to take care of her. I never saw my mother throw tantrums, yet when Margaret didn't get her way, she threw tantrums.

My mom had a difficult childhood. Her father was the tax-collector in Tallinn, Estonia—a difficult job, to be sure. I know little about him; however, I learned he often pulled my mother's hair and used other forms of corporal punishment to discipline my mother when she struggled with her studies. Apparently, my mother struggled with basic math, which brought on her father's disdain. After all, he was the local tax collector; his business was numbers.

My mother's mother was kind and compassionate, but she also had an abusive childhood. Her father was a tailor, and consequently, my grandmother worked as a seamstress. She learned a variety of skills from her father, but he also apparently abused her. This history of generational abuse would later affect my own life.

I recognize within myself qualities from both my parents. I like to think I received the best of both. Perhaps I believe this because of my birth order. I am the middle of three daughters. I am nineteen months younger than my older sister, Helen. It was a challenging time for my parents because my father had completed his work contract in Sherbrooke, Quebec. The young family was relocating to

Toronto, Ontario, in hopes of finding work. They moved in with my paternal grandparents shortly before I was born.

As a young child, I was reminded many times that I was the family accident. I was told my mother left me in a carriage outside a store when I was an infant. She walked away with my older sister in tow until my sister asked, "What about Tiiu?" My mother quickly returned to get me, but my older sister has often jokingly said my mother should have left me there. (Perhaps my abandonment issues stem from that event.)

In retrospect, I realize many forms of abuse exist that affect a child's self-confidence. Harsh words are powerful and can leave a lasting negative impression on anyone, especially young children.

My sister Margaret is nine years younger than me. When she was born, my parents were more financially secure and could provide a better life. In many ways, because of the large age gap between us, my younger sister was raised like an only child.

In researching the effect of birth order on a person's personality, behavior, and worldview, I discovered a variety of information. For the most part, in my opinion, the basic information is consistent across sources. Below are some of the birth order characteristics that were apparent in our family, although my younger sister does not fit the description. I believe because she is nine years younger than me, the closest sibling in age, she is almost like an only child.

In an article written by Penny Travers, "Birth Order: How Your Position in the Family Can Influence Your Personality," parenting expert and author Michael Grose said, "Birth order accounts for the differences between kids within families." It is common for parents to scratch their heads wondering why their firstborn and their second child are so different. In our family, my older sister and I were less than two years apart, we were raised the same way, and graduated from the same public schools, but we are as different as chalk and cheese.

In summary:

The first child:

- Is often a high achiever and leader.
- Is likely to be controlling and likely to take on responsibility.
- Is often a perfectionist and resonates best with other first-born children.

The second or middle child:

- Is likely the peacemaker, willing to go with the flow.
- Is often a good negotiator.
- Is likely to seek attention. Middle children will often have more friends in an attempt to compensate for the lack of family support.

The youngest child:

- Is likely to be more outgoing, independent, and charming. They thrive on attention but are more independent than their siblings.
- Is often given more freedom and subsequently has greater opportunities to try new things.

Family dynamics, birth order, and evolving parenting skills set a mental template of learned behaviors. As children mature and become adults, learned behaviors may become toxic patterns, even though the family members may feel the behaviors are normal. Many adults struggle with self-worth, lack of self-love, and low self-esteem. These patterns were instilled at a young age, so as adults, they don't necessarily realize their toxic behaviors stem from their childhood.

As a middle daughter born to immigrant parents with old-school child-rearing methods, I found that adapting to modern society frequently left me in conflict with what was expected. My parents had taught me that children are to be seen and not heard. I was often told to sit quietly and just listen. I was raised with strict discipline and corporal punishment, from a belt to a wooden spoon across the backside or across the hands.

As it is for many people, my childhood is a foggy memory. How old were you in your first childhood memory? As I mentioned before, my first memory is of visiting Niagara Falls. I had no idea at the time that Niagara Falls would be a pivotal location in my adult life.

Moving across Canada at age three was quite an adventure. I mostly remember the journey through the few photographs we took and the stories my parents told me over the years. I clearly remember the backseat of the old Pontiac. My father was always in a hurry to get to our destination, and at times, there were scary moments when I hid on the floor behind the driver's seat. I remember driving along the Fraser River Canyon with the edge of the road so close to the canyon; in some areas, barely enough room existed for two cars to pass on the two-lane, dirt roadway. In those days, seatbelts and child safety seats were nonexistent. Many a time, my mother looked over the seat to reassure me we would be all right. My sister Helen would often call me a big baby. But really, I was only three, so perhaps she was correct. I usually sat directly behind my mother, who would at times reach between the seat and door just to touch me and let me know she was watching out for me.

While I remember little about the drive, I do remember when we arrived at the house my maternal grandparents lived in. When they heard the old, two-tone, dark blue on top, light blue Pontiac stop in the driveway, they hurried outside. My father held me as my mom ran to hug her mother. I saw Dad and my step-grandfather, Isa, shake hands. It was a formal greeting, but then they enjoyed a beer together and shared stories about their cross-Canada journeys.

We lived in my grandparents' basement for a few months. The one thing I will always remember is the low beam at the top of the stairs. My father bumped his head on it many times and then would quietly mumble while rubbing his head. It was a little house full of love. My grandparents, my aunt, and the four of us found a loving beginning in a new city.

In retrospect, my memories are an interesting blend of the magical and the terrifying. Like my father, I am interested in aviation and classic cars. As a young child, I often dreamt I could fly, and in my heart and soul, I believed I would one day. As an adult, I have taken flying lessons and gone skydiving. Aviation still intrigues me. Preparing to jump out of a perfectly good airplane is a bit terrifying, but once airborne, the experience is indescribable.

By learning about spirituality, I have developed a greater understanding of the power of achieving harmony and balance in mind, body, and soul. The Universe has always called to me. As a child I would often gaze into the night sky and feel a strong connection to the stars and Orion. I believe my essence is a free spirit. I have learned that our souls incarnate into our bodies just before or right after our birth. Each soul has a mission (a purpose in life) and through our life experiences, we begin to identify our method, our plan for how we intend to fulfill our purpose.

My father had often considered a career as a pilot, but when he became a father, he changed his mind. He felt he needed a profession where he was safely on the ground. With his experience

building workshops and outbuildings on the farm and later working for a fellow Estonian builder, construction became his business.
Ironically, his career as a carpenter building single family homes led
to him falling off many rafters and rooftops. I'm glad he landed on
soft dirt piles and the occasional paint bucket. Despite some of his
work-related spills, he built beautiful homes in many communities
on Vancouver Island. On his days off, he was an avid fisherman. Isa
would often join him. They fished for trout on the local lakes and
salmon on the ocean waters. Thanks to their passion for fishing, we
were raised on a very healthy diet.

The 1950s was an age of housewives—women were homemak-
ers, spending their days caring for the family. My mother stepped
into that role proudly. Helen often demanded a lot of attention
from my mother, so I learned how to entertain myself.

I am not sure what compelled me to leave home, but as a four-
year-old, I began to defy rules and venture into my imagination.
One day, I grabbed my favorite stuffed toy, a plush yellow rabbit,
by the ear and walked away from the apartment on Hillside Road.

In the late 1950s, Hillside Road was a main road in Victoria, but
it only had two lanes and the traffic was minimal. I remember walking past the German delicatessen next to our apartment building.
My mother often took me to the deli. The man behind the counter
would chat in German with my mother and slip me a cookie. On
this particular day, I remember walking past the open door and him
smiling as I walked by.

The curb was a little high for me, and I remember someone
walking with me, helping me safely across the street. When I looked
back to say thank you, the man was gone. In retrospect, I wonder

if that man was my guardian angel. I have had many unexplainable experiences since that day.

I walked a few blocks to the small baseball field near another busy intersection. It was a beautiful day, and I took my socks and shoes off and ran barefoot in the freshly cut grass. I can still smell the scent of the grass as it tickled my feet while I was spinning around with my arms stretched out like eagle wings.

Soon after I started enjoying the freedom, I heard my mother frantically calling my name. I spun around and saw her running across the field. She was so glad to find me, but oh so upset. I was severely scolded and lovingly hugged at the same time. She scooped me into her arms, grabbed my socks and shoes, and ran frantically back to the apartment where a neighbor was watching over my sister.

In retrospect, I think Mom protected me by not telling my father what I had done. I know I would have remembered being punished. I believe the owner of the deli called our neighbor, who then told my mother. We did not have a telephone at that time. I remember the furnishings in our apartment were scarce and my sister and I slept on a mattress on the floor in a very small room.

Most of my childhood memories are like anyone else's. Some were happy; some were devastating; and some were curious. Helen often bullied me, pulling my hair, insulting me, and cutting the hair off my favorite dolls. When I complained, I was usually told to calm down and sit quietly, followed by more demeaning interjections from my sister and words I cannot echo that still ring in my memory. Words have an energy, and negative words can linger in our memories for decades.

One memory I need to share is the one I believe became my go-to safe place through many difficult times. My mother had gone to talk to our neighbor, Elaina. They were becoming good friends and spoke German together. My sister and I were eating lunch at the dining table. My father had built the table and chairs, which were painted a nice cream color. Many times, my parents had warned me not to rock in my chair. But being the curious risk-taker, the moment I heard my mother's footsteps going down the stairs, I turned the chair around and kneeled on it. I began rocking back and forth. I imagined it was a beautiful stallion running through a meadow. The wind was blowing through my blonde hair, and I could feel the fresh air caressing my cheeks. My sister's bossy voice was barely audible. I felt so free. It was awesome.

There was a sudden bang as my chin hit the table and the chair flew out from under me. I heard Helen screaming as she ran out of the apartment, "Boy, are you in trouble now! I'm telling Mommy!"

As I picked myself up, blood flowed out of my chin and splattered on the floor. I cried and grabbed my chin as I ran into the bathroom. I closed and locked the door as I slid with my back against the door to the floor.

Then, I felt someone knocking on the bathroom door—my mother. I was afraid to open it. Her comforting voice reassured me she was not angry; she just wanted to see if I was all right. I could hear her telling Helen to go sit down and finish her lunch. Slowly, I opened the door and let her into the bathroom. I remember her gentle touch and comforting words right before I blacked out. My chin was badly cut, and the remainder of the day is a blurred memory.

Mom told me years later that she called a taxi to take me to the hospital where a doctor stitched up my wound. I vaguely remember lying in the taxi's backseat with my head in my mom's lap.

Apparently, I had given myself a concussion. That stallion had certainly provided a wild ride for a little adventure seeker. Ironically, as fate would have it, today I own the chair, show off my first scar, and seek solace at times of duress in the comfort of my bathroom behind a locked door.

Through my spiritual growth, I have looked back and seen when God, the True Source, truly saved my life.

As we all know, God has many names. Knowing most have been used in vain, I choose to say God, the True Source. I say this with the utmost respect for everyone who believes in a Higher Power.

On Vancouver Island, on the west coast of Canada, is a beautiful area called Parksville. It is bordered by ocean and sheltered by mountains. When I was a child, my parents often took the family camping in a beautiful area close to the ocean beach. We would sit at the beautiful, sandy beach where the tide went a long way out and made the water shallow near an old pier. One particularly warm, summer day, my father blew up some old inner tubes and helped Helen and me take them out to the water where we were told to go and play.

I was an adventurous four-year-old that summer. My father told Helen to look after me and instructed us not to go too far from the shoreline. He told us to keep track of distance by a spot on the pier. I guess he knew the tide was coming in.

We had no concept of time, and I was enjoying my freedom, imagining a life as a mermaid, perhaps. Helen told me not to get too close to her. The waves were getting stronger, and I began slipping deeper into the water. I could no longer feel the sand under my feet, and I held tightly to the old brown rope my father had tied onto the inner tubes.

Helen started screaming. As my head slipped under the water, I saw my mother running up the beach toward us. I saw bubbles floating up to the surface as I struggled to hold onto the rope, thinking my mother would rescue me. I saw her pulling Helen up through the water as I began to lose my grip on the rope. The inner tube was floating away from me, and I was no longer holding on—just slowly sinking deeper into the water.

The bubbles began to disappear once I was no longer breathing.

At that moment, I felt something gently lift me up toward the inner tube floating above my head.

The brown rope touched my hand. I grabbed it and held on tightly as the inner tube began floating me toward the shore with a gentle motion that was stronger than the waves.

As I felt my feet touch the sand again, I gasped. I was finally able to stand up, and I saw my father running up the beach to help me. Slowly, I pulled the inner tube out of the water. My father picked me up in his strong arms and carried me back to where my mother was comforting my sister. Helen was hysterical. I just sat on a blanket wrapped in a towel.

I never told anyone what happened to me—how someone or something had rescued me. Everything we go through remains in our memory. As we get older and accumulate more and more memories, they often bury the events of our childhood. But this event was recently brought back to me. It was one of those moments of understanding. I realized while meditating that whatever had gently lifted my body from the powerful undertow so I could reach the rope wrapped around the inner tube was my guardian angel. Surely, there must be a reason that blonde-haired four-year-old was rescued.

Focus Questions

1. When you reflect on your childhood, what are some of the most memorable moments?

_____

_____

_____

_____

_____

_____

2. Whom did you look up to and why?

_____

_____

_____

_____

_____

_____

3. How did your parents discipline you?

_____

_____

_____

_____

_____

_____

4. Describe how were you compared to siblings.

_____

_____

_____

_____

_____

_____

5. How did your parents encourage you to try new things?

_____

_____

_____

_____

_____

_____

6. How were your parents supportive when you voiced your opinions?

_____

_____

_____

_____

_____

_____

Summary

Young children are a bundle of "curiosity" wrapped in "love." They give their love unconditionally, and only begin to withhold their emotions and personal growth when they begin to feel inferior or insecure. When children are raised in a nurturing environment, it is easy for them to thrive. However, if children hear harsh words, or they feel intimidated or embarrassed, they begin to lose self-worth and self-confidence. These small incidents create seeds of self-doubt. Consider the type of environment you had growing up. My parents often compared me to my older sister. They often expected me to have high grades in school, and when I didn't meet their expectations, I felt stupid, which fed my insecurities.

Chapter 4

Feeling Inspired by Helen Keller

Resilience

"Hope sees the invisible, feels the intangible,
and achieves the impossible."

— Helen Keller

During the spring of 1962, when I was nine, my parents let me watch the movie *The Miracle Worker*. This movie, about Helen Keller, would resonate within my heart throughout my life. I was inspired by her determination and wild temperament. The film shows Keller trapped in a lonely, confusing world of darkness and silence from infancy. She was born healthy on June 27, 1880, in Tuscumbia, Alabama. Due to an illness when she was only nineteen months old, Keller lost her sight and hearing. Young children learn how to navigate life by watching parents and siblings. They learn to speak by imitating the people around them. During her formative years, Keller was without vision and hearing. She had no idea how to express her needs. She had tantrums and behavior problems because she had no way to communicate.

Keller's family desperately reached out for help. In 1886, Keller's mother learned through an account in Charles Dickens' *American Notes* of a deaf and blind woman named Laura Bridgman who had been successfully educated. The quest began with Keller and her father traveling to consult with physician J. Julian Chisolm, an eye, ear, nose, and throat specialist. The doctor led the pair to Alexander Graham Bell, who was working with deaf children at the time. Bell referred them to the Perkins Institute for the Blind, where Bridgman had studied.

Attending school was a pivotal part of this story because Anne Sullivan, who was also visually impaired and would become Keller's teacher, was a twenty-year alumna of the school. Sullivan had contracted an eye disease when she was five, leaving her frightened and afraid. She could relate to how Keller was struggling. Sullivan had been abandoned by her father and sent to live in an over-crowded, underfunded group home. Anne Sullivan became Helen Keller's instructor, governess, and eventually, life-long companion. Sullivan's patient understanding and creative teaching skills were the catalyst that led Helen Keller to become an author, political activist, and lecturer.

Sullivan tried to teach Keller sign language by pressing her fingers into Keller's hand so Keller could feel the sign. After a few attempts, Keller would get frustrated and throw things. But Sullivan's consistent efforts and gentle ways won out. The breakthrough moment came when they were at the family water pump. Sullivan made the sign for the word "water" on Keller's palm while the cool water gently flowed over her other hand.

Keller recalled the moment in her autobiography, *The Story of My Life*, as follows: "I stood still, my whole attention fixed upon the motions of her fingers. Suddenly I felt a misty consciousness as of something forgotten—a thrill of returning thought; and somehow the mystery of language was revealed to me. I knew then that w-a-t-e-r meant the wonderful cool something that was flowing over my hand. The living word awakened my soul, gave it light, hope, set it free!"[1]

After watching the movie and reading the book, I was inspired by Helen Keller and researched more about her amazing life. She was a prolific author and outspoken in her convictions as she campaigned for women's suffrage, labor rights, socialism, and similar causes. Helen Keller was a member of the Socialist Party of America and the Industrial Workers of the World, and in 1971, she was inducted into the Alabama Women's Hall of Fame.

No matter what this young girl had endured, once she understood the importance of communication, she did not let her limitations stop her. Helen Keller said many inspiring words, and I have gained inner strength and insight from many of them. Keep this one in your memory: "Never bend your head. Always hold it high. Look the world straight in the eye." No one knows what the future holds; this fleeting moment is all you have, so live in it and be grateful knowing you did your best.

What I have learned from Keller's story is we need to adapt to what life throws at us and be resilient. We must not concede to the will of others. We have the ability to choose, yet so often, due to situations and experiences, we allow other people to manipulate our mindset. We must respect the opinions of others; however, we must trust our instincts to decide for ourselves what is best for us. Many people advised Keller's parents to put her in an institution. But

---

1. "Helen Keller's Moment." *The Attic.* https://www.theattic.space/home-page-blogs/2018/11/29/helen-kellers-moment. *The Attic.* Retrieved December 4, 2018.

her parents continued to search for someone who could help their daughter. Their love for their daughter kept them focused on their goal. When Anne Sullivan entered Keller's life, things improved. There are many examples of resilience in this story. In the end, Helen Keller and Anne Sullivan built a beautiful friendship that continues to enrich the world today. They faced many challenges in the early years, but they were resilient as they endured the years of learning.

"Don't let someone else's opinion of you become your reality."

— Les Brown

Focus Questions

1. In your childhood, were you groomed to be a certain kind of person? Explain.

_____

_____

_____

_____

_____

_____

2. As an adult, did you have a relationship where your partner did not respect your opinions? Give an example.

_____

_____

_____

_____

_____

_____

3. In your youth or as an adult, were you judged harshly by how you reacted to situations? Describe the judgment.

_____

_____

_____

_____

_____

_____

4. When you were judged harshly, think about how you reacted to that judgment. Did you get angry or fearful, or did you accept someone else's opinion of you without defending yourself?

_____

_____

_____

_____

_____

_____

Summary

The *New Oxford American Dictionary* defines "resilience" as "the capacity to recover quickly from difficulties." Think about how you reacted when faced with challenges. Did you freeze, fight, or flee? Many times when we struggle with low self-esteem, low self-love, or low self-worth, we lack critical thinking skills and react instinctively. Perhaps that reaction is a learned behavior from childhood. What if you didn't react but acted based on your thoughts?

Congratulations if you assessed the situation and were able to ebb and flow through the challenge. Rolling through the ebb and flow of life's energies is such an important act of resilience.

Chapter 5

Peace, Love, and Rock 'n' Roll

Trust

"The greater danger for most of us lies not in setting our aim too
high and falling short; but in setting our aim too low
and achieving our mark."

— Michelangelo

When Bob Dylan wrote his timely song "The Times They Are
a-Changin'," the United States was filled with social movements to
stamp out inequalities, including the Civil Rights Movement, the
Women's Movement, anti-war protests against the war in Vietnam,
and the Stonewall Riots, which were the catalyst for the gay rights
movement. These were times of much unrest, and thousands of
voices were speaking out for equal rights.

As a teenager growing up in a traditional family, my rebel side
screamed inside my soul. I experienced the devastation of the assas-
sinations of President John F. Kennedy, his brother Bobby Kennedy,
and Martin Luther King, Jr. I watched as we landed on the moon.
Volatility and scientific breakthroughs were behind so many historical events, which were brought into our homes via television.

We watched the Vietnam War presented on the nightly news, and for the first time in history, the sounds of gunfire and rescue helicopters and our armed forces were in Americans' living rooms. My father watched strategic battles while my mother busied herself in the kitchen. She did not want to be reminded of World War II. During the live broadcasts from the battlegrounds in Vietnam, when we heard the gunfire and bombs, I could see my mother flinching in the kitchen. She would turn the water faucet on and wash dishes to drown out the sounds. Sometimes we heard her drop a dish. I can only imagine the childhood flashbacks she must have suffered of bombs being dropped on Tallinn.

Then came Woodstock! It happened August 15-18, 1969. Woodstock was one of the most significant music festivals in history, and it continues to resonate with lovers of that era's music. The original location for Woodstock was changed because so many people showed up the facilities were inadequate. Regardless of locals' many concerns, Max Yasgur offered his dairy farm for the huge audience. The event took place in Bethel, New York, forty miles southwest of Woodstock. It was described as three days of peace and music.

At the time of Woodstock, I had just celebrated my sixteenth birthday. It was summer, and I had asked my parents if I could attend. My father's sister lived in Toronto and offered to take me to Woodstock. I was devastated when my father firmly said *no*. I was so upset and begged and pleaded with him to let me go. I knew it was a once-in-a-lifetime musical event, and many of my favorite bands would be performing.

My sisters and I were raised under strict rules, and our time was regulated. We had chores, homework, and specific times to be home. We had little free time to be with friends, so one thing I craved was to have a good friend. But I spent most of my time alone. With the constant berating from my older sister, and demands to take care of my younger sister, our sibling relationships were strained at best. My place of peace and comfort became the rocky cliffs overlooking the Pacific Ocean. I would often ride my bicycle down to the edge of the cliff and sit there for hours. I took comfort in the sound of the waves hitting the rocky coastline. Many a time, I wondered where the waters had traveled from, what stories they could share. As with everything on Mother Earth and in the Universe, water has an energy that carries a vibration felt on the planet and beyond.

I had been bullied in school. Being one grade behind my older sister, we attended the same high school. If I was in the same hallway between classes, Helen would tell me to stay away from her. She preferred that I avoid her without regard to any inconvenience for me. She told me I embarrassed her. Many teachers remembered Helen and would often say something like "We have another Napp girl; let's see if she's as smart as her sister." I felt I was already targeted for bullying, and it was just more fodder for the bullying that I was the big chested, skinny girl, with a funny name and weird accent. I was desperately trying to fit in somewhere, but it was an exercise in futility. Consequently, I often skipped classes and wandered into the hills behind the school. My grades suffered because I was absent much of the school year.

My senior year, I did have a boyfriend. He was a year younger than me, but we enjoyed our time together. We went on adventures in historic Victoria, and we spent many hours exploring museums. It felt wonderful to finally have a friend who loved me for who I was.

Now, I must be perfectly honest here. I was not the perfect young lady. Like all young adults, my boyfriend and I had to learn to understand our raging hormones. I was no different, but I got caught up with some of the wrong crowd. Use your imagination here when I say sex, drugs, and rock 'n' roll. Some of the choices I made led me to difficult decisions. Unfortunately, I fell victim to my poor choices and became pregnant soon after graduation. I continued to work and keep it a secret because I was living at home and knew my father would be furious. He already frowned upon my relationship with my boyfriend.

With all due respect to cultural diversity, I must admit my father was a bit opinionated about different cultures. He wanted me to marry a nice, young Estonian man, but in our tiny community there were few young men of Estonian heritage. To complicate potential teenage relationships, my father was strict on what race I could date. Perhaps he had envisioned my true love would have Estonian roots like I had. In my opinion, race is irrelevant because love is a matter of the heart, and in my mind, love is unlimited. My argument to my father was always that the color of a person's skin does not matter, because on the inside, we all bleed red blood. I'm sure my father was also concerned that I might get involved in difficult situations because of what had happened during the Civil Rights era. Race riots had been happening for years. My father felt I was too naïve and trusting.

"I look to a day when people will not be judged
by the color of their skin,
but by the content of their character."

— Martin Luther King, Jr.

I was asserting my independence, and I had many conversations about discrimination with my father. But today, I understand his concern for me. Much of it was related to his upbringing. In my mind, I have always felt that everyone is created equal. I have always believed we should all be treated equally—following the principles Dr. Martin Luther King, Jr. represented.

I was devastated when I watched the news reports of Dr. King's assassination. Like many other Americans, I continue to wait for true equality under the law and justice for all. Even today, after the tumultuous Civil Rights movement of the 1960s and the giant step forward it spurred, there is still so much separation.

During the 1960s, so many events were reshaping our world at that time, yet my parents struggled to be open-minded about what their daughters should be doing. I know my independent mindset was frightening to them because they wanted to protect me, but I often wonder where my life would have gone had they simply trusted my judgment. I knew my boyfriend had a good heart and would accompany me in moving in the right direction because his value system aligned with mine.

Then again, without my parents' strict oversight, perhaps my life would have been worse. I did trust people too quickly. But that was because I thought most people were trustworthy like me.

Focus Questions

1. Criticism by peers can leave long-lasting effects. Were you ever negatively judged? Describe.

_____

_____

_____

_____

_____

_____

2. Do you remember the words used by those who judged you and how you felt? List some words.

_____

_____

_____

_____

_____

_____

3. What did you do?

_____

_____

_____

_____

_____

_____

4. Did anyone step up to defend you? Describe.

_____

_____

_____

_____

_____

_____

5. Did your parents trust you to go out with your friends? Explain.

_____

_____

_____

_____

_____

_____

6. Are you someone who trusts people quickly, or do they need to earn your trust?

_____

_____

_____

_____

_____

_____

Summary

Merriam-Webster defines "trust" as "assured reliance on the character, ability, strength or truth of someone or something." In looking back at issues of trust in your past, did you see a pattern? Perhaps you found yourself constantly defending yourself or your decision. Or were you experiencing people who would say one thing and then do something else? In retrospect, I look at people today and ask myself, "Are they wearing a mask? Are they trying to manipulate my thinking?"

Chapter 6

Lost Love/Lost Lives

Discipline

"'Tis better to have loved and lost
than never to have loved at all."

— Alfred, Lord Tennyson

I struggled with telling my parents I was pregnant. I knew it would be another clash of opinions, and I had no intention of having an abortion to hide it from them. I was trying to exercise my free will under strict scrutiny from my parents, and the generations in our house often collided. Dad had strict rules; I had free will and a job. Mom always sided with dad, understandably. Helen threw more proverbial fuel on the fire by her own free will antics, and Margaret was also quite the handful.

In the summer of 1971, Helen moved to France. I knew little about her reasons for going to Paris, but I felt a sense of relief because she would no longer be bullying me. She was twenty years old and beginning a life of international adventures. Of course, that meant I became the primary focus of my father's strict guidance and opinions, and we did not agree on many subjects.

Things turned scary during my pregnancy because I suffered from abdominal cramps and bleeding. My obstetrician ordered bedrest. I didn't know how I would explain bedrest to my parents. I did my best to rest as I struggled with what I would tell them.

One night that dilemma went away. As fate would have it, my pregnancy ended with a miscarriage. It happened in the bathroom across the hall from my parents' bedroom while they were sleeping. Silently, I endured the pain and heartache as new life ended and left my body. This experience haunted me for decades until I finally found closure.

I did my best to clean up the evidence, but my mother came to me the following morning and gently told me she knew something had happened. I sat stoically, suppressing my tears, while my heart was breaking. She tried to comfort me by saying something was probably wrong with the baby, which was why my body miscarried.

I was never able to tell my boyfriend what had happened, and from that day forward, my parents would not let him near me. We did not have cell phones back then. We never spoke again, and for years, I thought he had abandoned me. Decades later, Margaret told me my boyfriend called many times, but my father would say I was not home, and I never got the messages.

I was so devasted by the miscarriage and not speaking to the baby's father that I ended up deeply depressed. I never had the opportunity to talk to my boyfriend, so I carried the burden of the loss alone. After the event, the topic was dropped, and I never sought medical care. Today, I wonder if the lack of medical care then had something to do with other health challenges I later endured.

During my depression, I followed the events happening in the world. I was trying to collect my thoughts and return to work. This was an era of many changes, and we felt them even in a quiet, small city like Victoria.

Racism was not much of an issue in our community. And I was a firm advocate for women's rights and equal rights for all. I understood those who came to Canada from the United States to avoid the draft. As a teenager, I hoped that when I fell in love, it would be with someone who had already served his time in Vietnam. I didn't think I would be strong enough to endure time away from the man I loved if he were fighting in a war. Today, I admire and have the utmost respect for all military families. Their sacrifices go far beyond the years of battles.

Medical advancements, the space program, and more innovations left everyone scrambling to share in the abundance of opportunities. Early computer systems were being introduced to schools while I was completing my final year of high school. The computer systems were operating only in the school through Intranet. I remember the computer room was filled with massive electronics. There were only a few computers in the entire school. The world was changing on many levels, and it was an exciting time to be a young adult. Unfortunately, my parents continued to suppress my curiosity and put restrictions on me as I graduated and worked three jobs in hopes of funding my independence.

I am not sure why my parents remained so strict and controlling. Perhaps because Helen had disrupted our family so often or because of the way my parents were raised. Either way, their old school, strict discipline was challenging for a young adult like me. I saw their rules as disrespectful of me as an adult.

After high school, I chose not to go to college because I wanted to study archeology and my father refused to fund my studies. He would only pay for me to study nursing or become a secretary—he would not fund my career "digging in dirt."

Today, I understand many professions in the past barred women. But at the time, I just burned my bra and became a free spirit!

Focus Questions

1. What stimulates your curiosity about the 1960s and 1970s?

_____

_____

_____

_____

_____

_____

2. How did your parents discipline you as a teenager?

_____

_____

_____

_____

_____

_____

3. Were you bullied or did you deal with peer pressure while a teenager? Describe.

_____

_____

_____

_____

_____

_____

Summary

It is important to have a disciplined mindset. There will always be times when people disagree; that's just the way life is. The problem I had for a long time was being afraid to speak my mind from fear others would disagree with me. Lacking self-confidence would often lead me into situations where I felt like the proverbial doormat. I have learned that not everyone will agree and that's all right. But we have to respect others where they are and also ask them to honor our opinion if it differs. In the 1960s, there were many episodes of people expressing their views and demonstrating for a myriad of equal rights. Imagine how our lives would have been affected if those individuals had not been disciplined in fighting for their cause? Whatever is going on in your life, decide and take action with a disciplined mindset for what you desire as the outcome.

Chapter 7

Hawaiian Connection

Love

"Sometimes no matter how hard we try,
things are just not meant to be."

— My Dear Mother

Soon after my miscarriage, my father offered to send my mother and me to Hawaii so we could spend time together and bond. I honestly did not want to go. But in my emotional turmoil, I decided it might be my only chance to explore Hawaii, so I agreed to the trip.

The flight was five or six hours. When my mother and I landed, we were greeted by locals with floral leis and an escort to the hotel.

The first few days were nice, but then things took a challenging turn. At our hotel, I met a young Vietnam veteran named Walter—his room was next to ours. We spent some time talking, and unfortunately, I began distancing myself from my mother to spend time with him. She had been smothering me with attention and we were doing only what she wanted to do. In all honesty, I was still reeling from the miscarriage and the loss of my one true love. This new man offered comfort and listened to my sad story with empathy.

When my mother caught me speaking to Walter at the pool, she said very sternly, "We need to talk, upstairs!"

I did not realize the power of words at the time, nor how they could resonate throughout a lifetime. That phrase, "We need to talk, upstairs!" would come back to haunt me for decades. The words triggered a reaction in my core that sent shivers through my body.

According to my spiritual coach, Dr. Michael Gross, who is a conduit for the power of the True Source, words have incredible power. Dr. Gross states:

> Every word has a frequency, vibration, and energy, which is electromagnetic and draws into your life whatever word you think and/or express. Negative words, thoughts, and expressions create in one's life fear, anger, anxiety, doubt, insecurity, hate, depression, pain, illness, and eventually, one's demise. Positive words, thoughts, and expressions create joy, happiness, abundance, prosperity, self-fulfillment, the achievements of one's dreams, healing, long life, and perfect health, and they enable your heart to sing. There is one word, and the expression of the word and emotion of the word will create, once again, the Garden of Eden on Earth. That word is love! Remember, you are created out of love, and from love, and that is your pure essence.

The tone in my mother's voice created a freeze, fight, or flight reaction in me. I refused to meet her in the hotel room. I literally fled—I ran away again.

I took off to hitchhike around the island of Oahu, but Walter would not leave me alone. It was frustrating. In desperation, I agreed to let him join me; after all, there is safety in numbers. At that point, I began feeling special and somewhat loved simply because he made me feel like I mattered.

We traveled the island for a few days, but we were eventually picked up by the police. It was hard to hide on an island. I was told if I didn't return to Canada on my return trip ticket, I would be in the country illegally and would be deported. Then I would never be allowed to return to the United States. I chose to leave voluntarily because I wanted to travel to the United States in the future.

The officers returned me to my mother at the hotel with instructions to be on the flight back to Canada the next day. Immigration would be watching. I talked to my father on the phone that night. He was glad the officers had found me, and he reassured me that he just wanted to talk to me when I got home. I knew he would do more than just a talk.

By that time, I was falling in love with Walter, but I thought perhaps it was just a rebound relationship because I felt very lost and needy.

Focus Questions

1. What was your biggest challenge as a teenager?

_____

_____

_____

_____

_____

_____

2. How did you overcome it?

_____

_____

_____

_____

_____

_____

3. Were you encouraged to speak your opinions and stand up and defend them? Describe.

_____

_____

_____

_____

_____

_____

Summary

The word "love" is hard to define because there are so many types of love. Sometimes parents exercise tough love. In retrospect, I know my mother had good intentions for me. However, sometimes people need others to be empathetic or compassionate. Teenagers facing major life decisions crave to be respected and not ordered to do things. When communications break down, there is no resolution, and I knew talking to my mother at that time would be non-productive. I was in the mindset of fleeing from any further conflict. When emotions run high, we sometimes seek comfort from wherever we can get it. That's why I allowed Walter to join me. Understanding that we may also experience misdirected love is important because if we don't recognize it, we end up making poor choices. We react based on emotion and not acting with intent.

Part II

Decisions

Chapter 8

Introduction to the Choices I Made

Self-Reliance

"If you think you can do it,
or you think you can't do it,
you are right."

— Henry Ford

During the final hours of my last evening in Hawaii, I stepped out onto the hotel balcony and was able to speak to Walter. I told him I had to return to Canada and handed him a piece of paper with my address. Honestly, I don't know why I did that, but I was afraid and desperate, and I needed to know I had at least one person in my corner.

On the long flight home, I was quiet and cried for hours. I knew my life was forever changed, and I was truly afraid of my father.

Upon our return to Vancouver Island, my grandfather picked us up at the small airport. I asked him why my father did not pick us up. He just shook his head as we quietly drove to the house. My grandfather pulled his small, yellow pickup truck into the driveway, but he did not come into the house. It was late, and I knew trouble was brewing inside. My grandfather had a sad expression in his eyes.

I walked through the carport, and as I opened the side door and stepped into the house, I saw my father standing in the doorway just inside the family room. He had his leather belt in his hands, and before my mother could step into the house, my father was striking me with the belt's metal buckle. I had barely put down my bags and taken off my coat. I could feel the buckle tearing up the skin on my back, my legs, and my arms. My father was yelling at me, and then I saw my mother come into the room. She scurried out another door with Margaret in tow.

I was devastated that my mother did not try to protect me.

I could see the rage escalating in my father's angry eyes. I did my best to defend myself as I tried to get to the kitchen and up the stairs to safety behind my bedroom door.

As I was running up the four steps into the kitchen, he grabbed my arm. I turned around and kicked him as hard as I could in his groin. He fell backward onto the floor, and I ran two steps at a time to the safety of my bedroom.

I closed the door and sat down with my back against it. I braced myself with my feet against the wall, for fear that he would try to get into my only safe place. I sat in the corner braced against the bedroom door, tears flowing down my cheeks, and realized I could no longer call this my home. This was no longer my safe place. All the trust, respect, and love I had for my father, my idol, spilled from my heart through my tears. After all the other losses I had endured, now my father was added to the list. He had been my hero and my protector—now he was someone I could no longer trust. My heart was ripping apart when I thought about my father. I had always looked up to him. I had trusted him to always love, protect, and understand me. I felt like my mother could not be trusted either because she focused on Margaret. It was as if sweet little Margaret could never do anything wrong. Yes, I know that sounds selfish, but Mom always defended her and protected her.

I could hear my father yelling and my mother trying to calm him down. In that defining moment, I made the biggest decision of my young life. Knowing my trust in my father was destroyed, I began planning to leave. I tried to find Richard, the father of my lost baby, but he had moved out of town, and no one knew where he went.

It would be many years before my relationship with my father was restored.

Recognizing that I no longer trusted my parents, I felt the only person I could trust was myself. I spent many days contemplating my options. It was a bittersweet feeling when I thought about everything that had happened—the miscarriage, the lost connection with my best friend, Richard, and the lost trust I felt with my parents. Clearly, I needed to become self-reliant and start a new life somewhere more promising than Vancouver Island.

During the following week, as I made plans to leave, my father and I kept our distance, and when we had to talk, it was minimal. I would politely excuse myself when my mother was not in the room. I continued to work and gather my paychecks.

No matter how loving we are, especially with our children, we all have a breaking point. We need to understand where the tipping point between raging anger and love is. What led up to that outburst? Where were my and my father's heads before the argument?

What events led to that state of mind? In the years following this traumatic lesson, I had to ask myself, "What was my part in it?"

Understanding my part in the argument was the beginning of forgiveness for everyone involved, including myself. I knew my father was looking out for my best interests, but his methods were disrespectful, ineffective, and brutal. They were certainly not appropriate for the society in which we lived at the time.

Focus Questions

1. Describe your relationship with your parents.

_____

_____

_____

_____

_____

_____

2. Was there mutual respect in your family? If so, describe it.

_____

_____

_____

_____

_____

_____

3. Describe the usual critical conversations with family members.

_____

_____

_____

_____

_____

_____

4. How did you cope when there was family conflict?

_____

_____

_____

_____

_____

_____

5. Did you have a safe place to go during family conflicts? Describe.

_____

_____

_____

_____

_____

_____

6. Did your parents encourage you to be self-reliant? How?

_____

_____

_____

_____

_____

_____

Summary

Self-reliance is often learned through interpersonal communications. When respect and communication break down, misunderstandings occur. This powerful altercation with my parents could have been handled in a more passive way had both parties had a mature discussion. Each person should have been given an opportunity to discuss their perspective and concerns with respect. Sadly, this scenario was a result of heightened emotions. The moral of this story would be: Never let negative emotions overpower love. Always remember it takes two people to create an argument. Granted, I was caught off guard, but what if I would have said, "Dad, I love you and I'm sorry"? Imagine how the outcome could have come out so differently. I highly recommend, "Always lead with love."

Chapter 9

Malibu Bound

Integrity

"The journey of a thousand miles
begins with one step."

— Lao Tzu

An example of strict (and ridiculous) discipline I experienced was my 10:00 p.m. curfew when my shift at the nursing home ended at 11:00 p.m. In addition, I paid rent and bought my own food, yet I was still grounded for not being home by my curfew. The unrealistic expectations solidified my goal of leaving home.

I was eighteen and naive when I moved out, and honestly, I did not plan my departure very well. I just packed my precious photos, birth certificate, and identification into my wallet, shoved a few articles of clothing and personal items into a backpack, and picked a day to walk away. What I took with me only got me through a few days. But I had also packed my courage and integrity, which would take me on an incredible, yet challenging journey.

I left a note. I kissed little Margaret on the top of her head as I sent her back to her room. It was early in the morning, and my parents were still sleeping. I quietly closed the side door and slung my backpack over my shoulder as I walked away.

My father and Helen had often argued during dinner. Frequently, tensions had escalated, and Helen had stormed away from the dinner table. There were times when I wanted to voice my opinions, but my mother tried to silence me with a gentle kick under the kitchen table when I tried to speak up. We had always been raised with the belief that children should be seen and not heard. When I did express my opinion as a teenager, my father would say, "You're a girl. What do you know?" My mother told me how much he wanted a son to carry on his family name. Sadly, that was not to be. His words echoed through my memories many times after I walked away from home. There were times I felt like a major disappointment to my parents.

On the occasions when I asked for my father's view on an issue, it was seldom a conversation. It was mostly his opinion, and since I was his daughter and not his son, my thoughts were seldom discussed. This type of relationship forced me to trust myself with difficult decisions. Unfortunately, some of my choices were spontaneous and not thoroughly researched. I lacked critical thinking skills, so it was easy for me to trust a man's opinion before trusting my own. But no matter how hard things got, I refused to compromise my moral values. My integrity remained intact no matter how hungry I felt.

I took a deep breath of fresh air as I walked up the road to the bus stop. I remember thinking, *Since no one would listen to me speak, perhaps now they will hear my message in the silence.* I had gathered final paychecks from my three jobs, and as I settled into the backseat of the bus, the weight of my world began melting off my shoulders. I finally felt liberated.

As I mentioned earlier I was very naïve, and my plans were poor. But we make decisions in desperate times by emotion—decisions we would never make with a clear heart and mind.

My new friend Walter, whom I had met in Hawaii, had arrived in town. I struggle now to remember how we reconnected. Anyway, he didn't have any money, but he said he would protect me because I was planning to hitchhike to Malibu, California. He assured me he had resources in California because he used to live in Huntington Beach. He said someone owed him money, and he had personal property stored at a friend's house. Having a traveling partner made perfect sense because I was only eighteen and naïve, and he was a Vietnam veteran. In my mind, I thought he would be a good body-guard on our journey south.

My goal was to go to Malibu and find a job working at a shop near the beach. California's culture, music, and artistic ambiance attracted me to look for my future there with like-minded, creative individuals. Unfortunately, to this day I have not made it to Malibu. In my naivety, I trusted the wrong people, and my California experience became traumatic in many ways.

The journey to California began as an exciting adventure. There was so much beautiful scenery to experience and enjoy. It really didn't matter that Walter and I often caught rides in the back of pickup trucks through twisting mountain roads. Klamath Falls, Oregon, will always be the moment I realized I was finally free from my toxic family. I began to feel a newfound freedom. My life was becoming my choice, and it was an exciting time in history.

My relationship with Walter was growing, and we shared our life stories. He had a colorful past. He was a slender man with wild, wiry, curly, dark-brown hair and brown eyes. He was about 5' 9".

He was five years older than me, and I was impressed by his life experiences. Walter had been married once and had two young sons living near Huntington Beach. Born in Redlands, California, he had grown up in Pennsylvania. I knew little about his childhood or why his family had relocated to Pennsylvania.

As the youngest of three brothers, Walter was the only one who served in the Navy. He said he was a radioman or communications officer. Most of his time in Vietnam was spent on the rivers near the frontlines. The servicemen who patrolled the rivers were often called River Rats. Walter shared stories of retrieving bodies from the rivers and facing enemy fire from the shores. As a radio operator, he was a target on the small boats patrolling the rivers. I was impressed by his cavalier attitude when telling many of the stories. I believe this attitude, shared by many who served, was a way of dealing with the human carnage he witnessed.

Walter told me one story about when the crew was using a fishing net to retrieve decomposing body parts from the rivers. Their mission was to bring these fallen soldiers home with an element of dignity. They were trying to retrieve a bloated corpse when its head rolled off the torso. They tried to retrieve the head and dog tags, but Walter couldn't remember what happened. He focused on their immediate task, which was making space in the cooler for the bodies until they returned to the main ship. Walter chuckled, remembering they had a lot of ice cream to eat before it melted in the heat.

One evening, Walter and I hunkered down for the night under a bridge on a hill overlooking a train track. We sat tucked into our sleeping bag. We were in northern California. As he started telling me one of his stories, I could see it was one he still struggled with. He had been on a trip like any other patrolling the river when suddenly the crew took fire from the brush on the shore. Walter radioed the command center, reporting they had been ambushed and were under fire. The gunfire briefly volleyed back and forth. He was in the wheelhouse with his friend Willie. Walter had just stepped down to get a better radio signal when shots directed at him struck Willie, who fell to the floor. Walter cradled his friend's head in his lap as Willie took his last breath. Walter shuddered as he shared the story, telling me he knew the bullet was meant for him.

As we fell asleep that night, I was worried I would roll onto the railroad tracks in my sleep, so I was restless. Sometime during the night, Walter let out a heart-wrenching scream. He jumped out of the sleeping bag, flipped over, and went headfirst back into the sleeping bag. He was screaming and crying. I put my hand on his back, and he began flailing inside the sleeping bag. I moved back away from him and calmly began talking to him. In my naïve effort to comfort him, I realized the best thing I could do was reassure him he was no longer in danger. He was safe with me. In time, I was able to help him slow his breathing and relax enough to get out of the sleeping bag. He crawled out. I helped him. Then I hugged him. I offered him water, but he just wanted his cigarettes. As he tried to light his cigarette, I could see how badly his hands were trembling.

That was the first time I witnessed the effects/symptoms of PTSD. So many Vietnam veterans returned home to a hostile reception. Walter was no different. It was protocol to travel in uniform, so many veterans were spit upon, berated, and ridiculed for serving in a controversial war. When Walter returned to the United States, he quickly changed into civilian clothing, but he brought within him two tours of duty riddled with violence and traumatic memories. Like many veterans, Walter carried within the silent parasite that often destroys the content of their character. Walter buried a lot of his pain in alcohol through the years we were together. He also struggled with authority and had a hard time working for anyone. Often, the stress of a simple short-order cook job at a diner became too much for him; then Walter would throw food across the kitchen. Sadly, he lost many jobs.

I became committed to doing my best to help Walter conquer his demons and find inner peace. In my heart, I knew he was doing his best to survive and adapt to life in 1972. Walter had served two tours in Vietnam honorably. In doing so, he had sacrificed so much of the young man he had been. He had entered the Navy at eighteen, which was close to my age when I met him. But when I was eighteen, I was a hippie and my motto was "Peace, love, and rock 'n' roll."

Walter's stories reminded me of *The Diary of Anne Frank*. I was inspired by her integrity as a young woman hiding with her family. Instead of having a bitter attitude about the situation, Anne continued to hold onto positivity and faith. Knowing a little about how my family escaped during World War II, I was drawn to absorbing Anne Frank's strength and tenacity.

When I met Walter, I had no idea how much I would have to depend on my own moral code and integrity. Our relationship was just beginning, and we had fourteen years of rough roads ahead. I made the personal decision to help him overcome his PTSD. We would have a daughter and a son. But unfortunately, with PTSD, you can only support and help those who suffer from it. Walter was not willing to do the work of conquering his demons, so I endured many forms of abuse over the years.

Focus Questions

1. List some words that create negative feelings in you.

_____

_____

_____

_____

_____

_____

2. How do you react when you hear them?

_____

_____

_____

_____

_____

_____

3. In our ever-changing world, who inspires you and why?

_____

_____

_____

_____

_____

_____

4. Did anyone ask you to compromise your moral codes? What did you do?

_____

_____

_____

_____

_____

_____

5. Do you know anyone who has experienced PTSD? How did
   they handle stress?

_____

_____

_____

_____

_____

_____

Summary

Integrity is having the ability to be honest and having strong
moral principles. Traveling with Walter opened my eyes to some
of the inequalities in life. When desperate times arise, our moral
codes and integrity are tested. How strong is your grip on your personal moral code? When you are challenged, is your belief strong
enough to keep you anchored? These are the times that impact our
self-worth, self-love, and self-esteem. Sadly, during this time, I did
compromise my integrity and carried the guilt for many years. I
understand now that we all carry karmic debt, and there is a way to
release the stresses of karmic debt.

Chapter 10

A Gun and Broken Promises

Courage

"Success is not final, failure is not fatal:
it is the courage to continue that counts."

— Winston Churchill

As I soaked in the old clawfoot bathtub, in the small house in Barstow, California, I trembled, tears rolling down my cheeks. I saw the blue sky of the warm day through the small window and watched the sunshine dance across the roses in the garden. I took in the modest bathroom with a glance. A little shelf near the sink supported a small, pink rose in a porcelain vase. The rosebud leaned toward the window where the sunshine was coming through, as if it were trying to join the dance in the garden.

The house belonged to Walter's grandmother. We sought refuge there after the recent trauma we had experienced in Orange County. It was very peaceful, which was welcome after our long road to safety. Sadly, as I scrubbed my body, I struggled to feel clean again. I could feel my soul shrinking deeper into my core.

Walter and I had arrived in Huntington Beach a few days earlier. He was connecting with his friend Sam to collect a debt. I was not part of the deal, so I had stayed back and waited across the street. Walter had taken my backpack with my few worldly possessions and said he would put it in a safe place. I saw my backpack disappear into the trunk of a car. Walter reassured me we would come back later to retrieve it.

We hitched a ride to another person's house. My memory is a bit vague here because we had not had a meal in three days, and we really had not slept much, but it was somewhere in Huntington Beach, or at least in Orange County. A man in his late thirties stopped and offered us a ride in his old pickup truck. He told us he just needed to make a quick stop at a friend's house and then we would be on our way. It seemed he was gone for a long time, so I put my head on Walter's shoulder to take a nap.

I woke up to the feeling of cold, sharp metal on my neck. I opened my eyes and realized it was the jagged blade of a knife. My elbow struck Walter's arm quickly, and I saw a gun pointed at Walter's head. His eyes were wide open in fear. Knowing he struggled with PTSD, I can only imagine how he was feeling staring down the barrel of a gun.

The man sitting in the driver's seat continued to point the gun at us while he placed the knife under his left leg, out of our reach. As I sat in the center of the bench seat, my mind processed what the future would hold for us. In all honesty, I kept hoping Walter, who had promised to protect me, would do something when the truck slowed down. My options were limited because the gun was aimed at me, and I had no way to get out of the truck. I was trapped. The man who had picked us up was upset that things had not gone as he had planned when he went into the house, while we waited. He began driving the truck along residential streets, I looked for a way to signal for help. But the road had little traffic, and in a few short minutes, we were traveling down an empty country road. Time was running out as the man turned into a dirt driveway that led to an abandoned building surrounded by acres of vacant land, brush, and trees.

The man stopped the truck, turned off the engine, and pulled the keys out of the ignition. He made us get out of the truck while he kept the gun pointed at us. He kept his hand on my arm as he ushered Walter into the abandoned brick building. There were only a few windows in the building. It looked like an old warehouse. It had high ceilings, bars across the windows, and some rusty equipment. The man left Walter in the building with no possible way to escape once the heavy metal door was barred from the outside.

I knew my survival depended on me.

The grip around my forearm became tighter as I was pulled into an empty field. I could feel the knife against my side. The stranger had pulled a small, light blue blanket from the truck. I had wrapped it around me earlier, when I was sleeping in the truck. He threw it on the ground.

My heart raced. I knew what his intentions were. I knew no matter how hard I fought, he was physically stronger, but I fought anyway. I was finally pushed onto the blanket. I chose not to scream for help because the only one who would hear my pleas was locked in the cold, impenetrable brick building. I chose to fight my own battle and not let him control my emotions. Screaming would give him the satisfaction of knowing I was afraid. My assailant became impatient and more aggressive. But I struggled to maintain my self-control and dignity.

The image of the gun barrel aimed at my head will forever be engraved in my memory. I continued to struggle, and at one point, I knocked the gun out of his hand. It fell by my side, and I grabbed it.

Suddenly, in a last effort to protect myself, I pointed the gun at his chest and pulled the trigger.

Nothing happened.

Then he grabbed the gun from my hand and told me the safety was on.

I was devastated because I knew what was about to happen. In remembering this, I believe I chose to mentally separate myself from the assault.

I became another statistic. The only saving grace was that Walter witnessed the attack and remembered the physical description of my assailant. My memory blocked some painful memories so I could endure the assault. Over time, the details of the attack have become blurry. But the one thing I will always remember is I defended myself more than I ever thought I could.

Despite the results of the attack, I am grateful the safety was on the weapon. My soul did not want me to become a killer—even in self-defense. Every life is important, no matter how twisted the person might be.

When it was over and the assailant was satisfied, I thought he'd leave us in the field. But he sent me back to the truck and released Walter. He got in the truck. I sat quietly, deep in thought about what I should do next. My emotions were like a rollercoaster. I was devastated, relieved, and disappointed that the one person who had promised to protect me had left me in the hands of the attacker. Walter had not even fought to stay out of the warehouse. He had fallen from grace in my eyes. My trust in him was shattered.

The assailant drove us to the outskirts of town, and we quickly got out of the truck. For some reason, I grabbed the blue blanket. We found a sheriff's office. My memory is foggy on this, but I vividly remember having to describe in detail what happened to me to several people. Reliving every detail was painful, and experiencing the collection of evidence for a rape kit pushed me into a state of emptiness within my soul. They asked so many questions that I felt like I was being violated over and over again. At times, they made me feel they did not believe me, or they implied that perhaps I had invited the assailant to take advantage of me.

For many, many years—and still today, really—the legal system has lacked compassion and empathy. For me, it was important to report the assault in hopes no other young woman would go through what I had just experienced.

Officials said they needed to keep my clothing, but I told them I did not own anything other than what I was wearing. Everything had been taken from me. The blue blanket and my underwear became evidence. As I walked out of the facility, I tucked my hands into my empty pockets. I felt completely broken.

Walter told me he would get me to his grandmother's house in Barstow. I really did not care where I went. I asked Walter not to tell his grandmother what had happened. We walked in silence for a bit. Then I asked him to promise he would not tell a soul. I just wanted the whole ugly memory to go away.

We hitchhiked to his grandmother's house. She welcomed us with open arms. We were hungry, tired, and dirty. The only thing I wanted to do was soak in a bathtub. As I slipped into the warm, soothing water, I looked back on the day, wondering why I was still alive. Looking at the barrel of a gun, surviving such an invasive assault, and losing trust in so many people almost destroyed me.

I heavily scrubbed my body, but it just would not feel clean no matter how long I sat in the tub of water.

I lost track of time, and the water became cold.

I finally got out and got dressed in some clean clothes Walter's grandma provided. When she left to put my clothes in the washer, Walter told me he had told her what had happened.

At that moment, I knew the only person I could trust was myself. I was devastated and empty because the only person I thought I could trust had broken his promise and did not respect my privacy. In retrospect, that should have been a red flag for me, but in the morning, I forgave him.

Focus Questions

1. Have you experienced a life and death situation? Describe it.

_____

_____

_____

_____

_____

_____

2. How did you handle it?

_____

_____

_____

_____

_____

_____

3. Have people broken promises to you? Give a brief explanation.

_____

_____

_____

_____

_____

_____

4. How did the disappointment make you feel?

_____

_____

_____

_____

_____

Summary

There are times when we don't realize our own courage and strength. When we are in danger, we enter a survival mindset. At those moments, we only have time to trust our gut instincts, not thoughtfully act. Many times, victims will freeze, fight, or flee. When considering your own personal life experiences, consider how you acted. Did you take control, or did you take on a victim mindset? Considering the situation in this story, my only goal was to survive. Courage kept me alive, and even though my body succumbed to the attack, my mindset stayed strong.

Chapter 11

Crossing Canada Alone

Perseverance

"How often I found where I should be going
only by setting out for somewhere else."

— R. Buckminster Fuller

After spending a couple of days with Walter's grandmother, I felt it was time for me to head north to Canada. My California dreams had been crushed. The backpack containing all my precious possessions was forever lost. When I asked Walter if we could retrieve it, he gave a resounding "no." I'm not sure what happened in Huntington Beach, but at this point, I just wanted to go back to Canada. I felt that at least in Canada, I could find a job and some housing and begin getting back on my feet. Once again, Walter said he would travel with me and protect me. I choked back a laugh and decided I would just send him back when I made it safely to the land of my birth.

Walter and I experienced more challenges on our journey, but perhaps I will write them in another book. Walter's grandmother had given us a little money and some sandwiches. We headed to Vancouver, but we were sidetracked at Lethbridge, Alberta.

Throughout the trip, I had been uncertain about what I wanted to do. I knew I did not want to go back to my parents' house, so we continued traveling northeast.

Walter insisted we should go to Pennsylvania where his parents lived. He knew where he could get work, and we would finally be able to stop hitchhiking across the continent. We decided to cross the border just south of Lethbridge, travel across Canada, and find a place to return to the United States. But as life would have it, when we attempted to cross the border into Canada, Walter, being an American citizen, was denied entry. To compound the issue, I couldn't reenter the United States because I didn't have any money.

Bus stations had become our go-to meeting places if we got separated while traveling, so I looked for a bus station where I could sit and consider my options. Before I got away from the border crossing, I saw Walter sitting in the backseat of a Canadian Border Patrol car. He had been caught trying to jump the border into Canada. What in the world had he been thinking?

When I returned to the border patrol office, I was told Walter was going to jail and would be in court in the morning. Once again, I was alone without the person who had promised to protect me. After a few minutes of despair, I considered my options. I was low on money, so I found an employment center. My plan was to find a place where I could do some work in exchange for a place to sleep. Sleeping in parks on benches or alleys behind dumpsters had become old, and it was autumn. The weather was getting very cold at night.

Fortunately, I found an ad for a live-in nanny for a toddler. I made a phone call and was invited to the house to meet the family. When I knocked on the door, a very tall man answered. He reached out his hand and introduced himself as Walter Mason. The irony of his name caught me by surprise. Soon, a very gentle Asian woman came around the corner carrying an adorable little toddler. Her name was Elsa, and we had an instant connection. I knew how to care for this beautiful child because I had experience caring for my younger sister. I was thrilled to have a place to stay and such a sweet child to care for.

Finally, at least for a little while, life was improving. At Walter's court hearing, he was sentenced to three weeks in jail and voluntary deportation for trying to illegally enter Canada. As sad as it was, I was grateful I had found a family where I was sheltered, fed, and had a sense of purpose, albeit if only for a few weeks. My days were spent caring for Elsa and visiting Walter in jail when time allowed.

When I found I was pregnant with Walter's child, after everything that had happened, I felt so many emotions! Nothing was more precious to me than carrying a new life within my body, but I was thinking, *How in the world will I provide for this blessed gift?*

When I learned Walter would be released and have to return to the United States the next day, I was still struggling with what I should do. I could begin a new life in Lethbridge, caring for Elsa indefinitely. I remember sitting on the floor in a small room, trying to decide. My life was such a mess, and I was trying to make some enormous life decisions. I was nineteen years old, pregnant, and in an unfamiliar city with nothing to my name. I considered my options. My unborn child was my main concern. I had to decide what was best for this new life. I decided I had three options:

1. I could continue to care for Elsa. I enjoyed caring for her, and her parents had offered me an opportunity to stay and be part of their family until I chose to move on. It was a beautiful option.

2. I could return to my parents until the baby was born. This option was my worst-case scenario.

3. I could stay with Walter, and we could begin a life together as new parents. This option felt right because I wanted my child to have both parents in their life. This would be the most challenging option because I knew Walter was no longer in the same country trying to protect me.

In my young, naïve mind, faced with a decision that would mold my entire life, I fell back on what I had learned in childhood. Family values and moral codes kept flowing through my mind. What I overlooked were all the red flags that had appeared in my short time with Walter.

What stuck in my head was my father saying, "You made your bed. Now lie in it." As his voice reverberated in my mind, I knew returning to my parents was no longer an option. Scratch that idea.

As I sat on the floor in the corner of my room rubbing my stomach, I knew I had to make a decision. Walter was being released into the US in the morning, and I was going to the jail to visit him and tell him my decision. After looking at the pros and cons of both options, I felt a strong urge to stay right where I was, with Elsa and her parents. But I lacked the self-confidence to be a single mother. My greatest struggle was I did not want to put my newborn into the hands of daycare workers while I tried to provide for my child.

My father had instilled strong family values in me. I knew that even though Walter had not proven to be trustworthy, he had a right to be in his child's life. So, I knew I had to try to connect with Walter. When I visited him in jail, I told him my decision, and we made plans to meet in Niagara Falls on the American side at a bus station. Walter's parents lived in a small town in Pennsylvania, and he was familiar with the bus station on the American side of Niagara Falls. He felt it would be easy for me to find.

When I told Elsa's parents of my decision, they were understanding and supported me. They also told me if I changed my mind, I was always welcome to return—they were truly a gracious and kind family. They paid me what I had earned, cautioned me about the risks, and the next morning, I said my farewells with a heavy heart. Caring for Elsa and the love I felt from her amazing family will always be a treasured memory. Sadly, we did not stay in contact.

My difficult decision was complicated by logic and reason. Any other confident woman in my situation—well, she would not have been in my position, but if she had been, she would have made a different decision. But I made the best decision I could, and I really do not regret my choice. I believe it was my destiny, even though many difficult years were ahead for me.

My most courageous journey began, step by step, as I walked away from the safety of the comfortable Mason family home. The road before me would be filled with many challenges, and all I could do was pray for the safety of my precious unborn child. The fall air was brisk as I pulled up my collar and adjusted the small backpack containing my few possessions. My money was limited because I had put some of it in an account at the jail for Walter so he would be able to get some food once in the USA. With only a small amount of money remaining, I tried to be frugal and planned to hitchhike to Niagara Falls.

The journey from Lethbridge, Alberta, to Niagara Falls, New York, was 2,100 miles along rugged roads, past truck stops, and through deep winter snows. I will never forget the bone-chilling cold I felt when trying to catch a ride, only to have the big semi-trucks drive past me. It felt like the wind cut through to my core—the tears froze on my cheeks, and I could no longer feel my fingers or toes.

The days began to run together, and I barely slept or ate. One late night, somewhere in Manitoba, I stopped at a diner to warm up and have a bowl of soup. I was down to my last $3.00, and I still had a long way to go to reach Niagara Falls.

It was almost 2:00 a.m. The waitress came to collect payment and tell me the diner was closing. A young man and I were the only ones left in the diner. He appeared to be traveling like me. As we gathered our backpacks and the diner door was locked behind us, we began chatting. We looked around in the meager light and realized there was no traffic and nowhere to sleep.

As we stood on the diner steps, he said, "I have an idea." Since my idea reserve was empty, I was open to it. Across the two-lane highway was a large, fenced, snow-covered field. He said we were in survival mode, and to survive the below-zero temperature, we should both get into one sleeping bag so our body heat would keep us warm.

I stepped back, a bit shocked, but the idea made sense. He reassured me we would stay clothed—it was the only option that appeared safe. Trying to hitchhike and stand on the dark roadside was dangerous because drivers would not see us. The diner's lights had been dimmed. After a few minutes of thinking it over, I accepted the invitation because I was shaking in the cold, and it was my best choice, my only choice.

This kind traveler was in his mid-twenties and had a caring demeanor. We hurried across the frozen highway. Then he found a small opening in the wire fence and held it open for me to squeeze through. He used a flashlight and found a relatively level spot. He spread out some plastic and placed the sleeping bag on it. It was incredibly cold, so I welcomed the feeling of warmth as our body heat began to fill the sleeping bag. I soon dozed off.

It was a long overdue sleep.

The sound of traffic on the highway woke us. It had snowed through the night, so we had at least a foot of snow on top of us.

We looked up—and jumped when we saw a rather large bull standing over us, his horns pointing down. We scrambled out of the sleeping bag and grabbed our stuff before hurrying through the opening in the fence.

When we reached the highway, we said our goodbyes and expressed our gratitude to each other. He was going west, and I was traveling east. I never asked his name, and when I looked back, he had disappeared. I have no idea if he got a ride or was simply someone sent by God, the True Source, to keep me safe.

Soon after, a large semi-truck picked me up, and my long trek continued.

After several days of traveling, I finally arrived in Niagara Falls. I stopped at a convenience store to ask where I could find the bus station. In 1972, there was no internet, no cell phones, just pay phones—we still had phone booths all over. Walter had estimated how long it would take me to travel to the destination, but we knew it would be random because I was hitchhiking. We agreed to stay and wait for each other. He planned to contact his family from Niagara Falls once he found me. He gave me their phone number in the event I couldn't find him.

But I hesitated to call because I had faith that we would find each other at the bus terminal. As any young woman lured by the thought of love, I felt he would be waiting there for me, and we would rush into each other's arms like in a Hollywood movie.

When I finally arrived at the bus station, only a few people were milling around. I walked around to see if he was around a corner or out back having a cigarette. He wasn't there.

I found a payphone and reached into my pocket for the last of my coins. Before I could deposit the coins, I heard someone call my name. It was a distant voice, but as I turned around, I saw Walter rushing toward me.

I stood frozen, relieved, yet apprehensive because of all the uncertainties. When he got closer, my feet moved me toward him, and we reached out for one another and a long-awaited hug.

Finally, my long, lonely journey had come to an end. Once again, we would travel together. This time we had a destination—Robesonia, Pennsylvania, where Walter's parents lived—and Walter knew the way.

Focus Questions

1. Name one thing you were determined to do, no matter what obstacles lay ahead.

_____

_____

_____

_____

_____

_____

2. What was your "why," your reason to keep going?

_____

_____

_____

_____

_____

_____

3. How did you complete the one thing?

_____

_____

_____

_____

_____

_____

4. If you didn't complete it, what stopped you?

_____

_____

_____

_____

_____

_____

Summary

No matter what the challenge, it is important to know your "why." When you know why you are focused on overcoming your fears and going after your goal, you are exercising perseverance. If you don't have a clear purpose for your goal, it is very easy to quit before you even get started. I knew that traveling across Canada would be risky and scary, but I knew my "why." My unborn baby needed to be with her father. That is what kept me going when I got scared, hungry, and tired. I kept believing my courage was just beyond my fears.

Chapter 12

Proclaiming Your Rarity

Trust

"Never, in all the 70 billion humans who have walked this planet since the dawn of time has anyone ever been exactly like me."

— Og Mandino

We finally arrived at Walter's parents' home. At first, I was a bit surprised when their welcome felt polite but distant. It took me a while to realize his parents felt obligated to take us in; they were disappointed that Walter had come home asking for help. Walter was still struggling to build a secure future with work and a new life after Vietnam. He had been married once and had two sons living with their mother in California. I guess that should have been a warning to me since he had no desire to be a father to his two sons. He said they were better off without him.

Walter's parents' home was temporary because they were moving into Walter's paternal grandmother's house with two cousins. Grandma had a large farmhouse on several acres and was no longer able to take care of herself. She was living on the lower level of the house because she was in a wheelchair. Walter's parents were going to live in the upstairs rooms. The cousins were living on the main floor, caring for Grandma.

Our time with Walter's parents was limited. Once again, I felt awkward and kept worrying about how we would care for our baby.

Walter decided we would be better off finding our own place. We found a tiny room in an old rooming house in Myerstown, Pennsylvania. He got a job at a factory that manufactured concrete castings. Our room was so narrow that a single bed barely fit between the walls, and we had to share a bathroom with the other residents. We cooked our food over a hot plate, and occasionally, we ate at the diner across the street. We did not own a car, so we walked everywhere, but the town was small, with only one traffic light.

We searched for better accommodations suitable for a family of three. After a few weeks at the rooming house, we found a small, one-bedroom apartment in an old house. It seemed nice considering what we could afford. The owner had even recently added wood paneling on the walls—the height of style in the '70s.

Every step since I left home had been challenging. The first night in our new apartment, I prayed and gave so much gratitude to God for saving my life. I could finally enjoy the last few weeks of my pregnancy and prepare for the arrival of our newborn. We had no idea what gender our baby was—all I hoped for was a healthy child.

Through the years, this passage from best-selling author Og Mandino has continued to remind me of the incredible miracle of life:

Today, I count my blessings and proclaim my rarity for I have learned that never, not among all the 70 billion humans who have walked this planet since the dawn of time, has anyone ever been exactly like me.

In a moment of supreme love, more than 400 million seeds of love flowed from my father, swam within my mother, and all perished except one—*me*.

I persevered, searching for my other half. The single cell from my mother—so small it would take 2 million to fill an acorn shell—against all odds, joined with the seed to begin a new life.

Through all the combinations beginning with the one single sperm from Dad's 400 million and through the hundreds of genes in each of the twenty-three chromosomes from Mom, 300 thousand billion humans could have been created each different from the other. I was born, one of a kind, a miracle! I am made of the four basic elements of life—fire, water, earth, and air. I take water to quench my thirst, and food grown from the earth to ease the hunger and give me strength. I breathe air to fill my lungs and give me oxygen, and I use fire to warm my body.

I have passed through infancy, adolescence, and am in my prime planning for the golden years. I have learned how there are many sets of fours. Four directions—north-south-east-west—four seasons—four basic food groups—four chambers of the heart (two go into and two go out).

Life is a fragile miracle, unique in every way. Consider this: Everything is an energy, every fingerprint is unique, and no one has identical DNA. How we view our rarity is a bit of an oxymoron because most people yearn simply to fit in. They fail to embrace their uniqueness.

As a mother, I understand the precious miracle of life. I did my best to bring a healthy infant into the world despite our living situation.

Life is a fragile miracle created from love and of love. While awaiting the birth of our first child, I silently prayed my newborn would be healthy. Walter and I had struggled with having enough food. Many times our diet was poor because we lacked money. I knew how precious the miracle of life is, so I wanted to give my child a healthy beginning. I later learned that the fetus would take what it needed to grow and develop from my body if my diet was poor.

Research indicates that in the last ten weeks of development, a fetus is learning and experiencing different sensations. A recent Parent Circle report states that five important things are learned while a fetus is still in the womb. Each experience the fetus has is creating their unique life experiences.

- They become sensitive to sound.
- Touch and feel sensations become evident.
- They learn elements of their first language.
- They begin signs of emotions such as smiling, crying, blinking, and frowning.
- The sense of taste is being developed based on what the mother eats and how it comes through the amniotic fluid.

As we know, we are all unique in many ways. Our bodies, living environments, and life lessons are all different, which makes me wonder, *Why do so many people want to be like other people?*

Focus Questions

1. Describe what is unique about you.

_____

_____

_____

_____

_____

_____

2. We are our biggest critic. How would you describe yourself as a critic?

_____

_____

_____

_____

_____

_____

3. Why would you compare yourself to other people?

_____

_____

_____

_____

_____

_____

4. What do you think makes you different?

_____

_____

_____

_____

_____

_____

5. Are you content with your life or are you still looking for your perfect life? Explain.

_____

_____

_____

_____

_____

_____

Summary

Many of us compare ourselves to other people we admire. We measure our success based on others' success. But do you realize the qualities we admire in others are usually the qualities we don't see in ourselves? Remember, like attracts like, and once we realize that, we begin to trust our own feelings. It's time to stop sabotaging yourself and trust and respect the true person inside. Listen to your inner voice; it will guide you to discovering your beautiful rarity.

Chapter 13

A New Beginning

Love/Loyalty

"In the end, only three things matter:
how much you loved,
how gently you lived, and
how gracefully you let go of things not meant for you."

— Gautama Buddha

In reflecting on my life, the birth of my daughter Emma in 1973 will always be one of my most treasured memories. The birth of my son Roger in 1975 was another incredible blessing. Both of my children have enriched my life in so many ways. I have a special place in my heart for each of them. The firstborn forever changes us, transforming us into parents. Becoming a mother was an awakening. My children are unique, and I am so grateful that their souls chose me as their mother. I have learned that our souls choose to incarnate into our human bodies to learn life experiences. As we grow through life, we get those gut feelings about the choices we make; it's our soul guiding us. My children are as unique as night and day, but both of them saved my life and continue to teach me. I am so very blessed that they came into my life.

We are aspects of God, the True Source, which is the energy of unconditional love. Late in my first pregnancy, as I gently rubbed my protruding stomach, I remembered my miracle child was created in a moment of unconditional love. Nothing is more powerful than *love*! I had read many books on how my precious baby was developing, and I yearned to hold this blessing in my arms.

Labor pains began early one morning. We made a trip to the hospital only to be sent home because I was in the very early stages. Later in the day, Walter went for a job interview in Harrisburg, Pennsylvania, thinking there would be enough time for labor to progress. I was alone in the apartment when the pain became intense, and my water broke. I was afraid he wouldn't get back in time and I would have to get help from the neighbor. Fortunately, I heard his car in the gravel driveway, and I got to the top of the stairs, bag in hand. I told him we needed to get to the hospital. After twenty-three hours in labor, I began to understand the power of love and how much the human body can endure. I knew everything I had been searching for was within my soul. It was time for me to trust the voice within to raise this beautiful gift from God, the True Source, to the best of my ability. This would be an incredible journey with my sweet child. I had such tender dreams of how life would go with children and grandchildren. My heart was full of love as my body contracted with pain. There were no expectations, only dreams and goals for a brighter future, enriched with the love and joy of a newborn child.

I only wish I would have taken my own advice in those days. *Stop looking for love in all the wrong places! It's not in other people or things.* I had such expectations that my child would finally give me the love I so dearly needed. What I have learned since that day is *love* is just beyond your fears. To move forward, we must step out of our comfort zone, move through our fears, and step into our abundant lives. Unconditional love is only one heartbeat away. But you, and only you, must decide to take the action. No one else can do it for you.

Unfortunately, we often allow others to tell us what we should do. By trusting others more than our inner voice, we often fall into pits of despair. At that moment, I found myself feeling lost and alone, hoping that once I held my precious child, life would improve, and I would finally feel loved.

I remember times when I brought up the subject of marriage. After all, we were preparing to welcome our newborn into the world. Walter would get annoyed, and the topic would get dropped. I knew Walter had been married before, but it would be years later when I learned he had not filed for divorce.

When we arrived at the hospital, Walter was shown to the waiting area and I was checked in and taken to a labor room. As I stood in the doorway of the room, it felt cold and empty. It contained two small beds, one against each wall, and a single window in the center opposite the doorway. A sharp pain squeezed my stomach into a knot, and my lower back pain was getting worse. I leaned against the door frame until the sister-nurse pointed me to a bed on my right. The bed was a small mattress on an old bedspring. The frame was of heavy metal painted a pale green, and it was covered with scratches, reflecting much use.

Through the window, I could see a brick wall and a narrow alley. The pain in my stomach was getting worse as I sat on the edge of the bed. When I had checked into the facility, I had been given a gown and thin blanket. It was time for me to change into the plain cotton gown and put my clothing into a bag. The aide put my name on the bag and left the room with all I had brought with me.

My pains increased, and I lay down to get some relief. The room's only adornment was a picture of the Virgin Mary. It was a hot, muggy day in June 1973, in Lebanon, Pennsylvania. The simple sterile room seemed appropriate but was nothing fancy. The nurses and aides were members of a convent. I would have many hours to look at the room and walk the hallway alone. My physician was old-school, so no one was permitted to visit while I was in labor.

Nineteen, naïve, and insecure, I was in labor with my first child. Alone! In a sterile, cold, empty, and lonely room. I knew little about the labor process and even less about what to expect during delivery. In 1973, expectant fathers and family in the labor room was a new concept that had been introduced in more liberal-minded facilities. Unfortunately, I was not in one of them.

As a single mother, I felt shunned to an extent. During labor, the nurse checked on my progress periodically, but she was very systematic and quick, not very personable.

Other women would occupy the other bed in the room, and within a few hours, they would be in the delivery room across the hall giving birth. I would hear the newborn babies cry and much excitement, and then someone would come and clean the neighboring bed. Before long, another woman would occupy the bed and move on to the delivery room. This happened three times, so as a first-time mother, I wondered what I was doing wrong, especially as my labor reached twenty-three-and-a-half hours.

I had no coaching or guidance on what to do. The nurses just said walk, suck on ice chips, and be patient.

Sex and everything related to it—including pregnancy and childbirth—was so hush hush back then that when I was growing up, my mother just handed me a book about sex and said, "It's time you read this." By then, I had already learned about sex in a special class in high school. I chuckle a little now remembering that when my younger sister was born, my mother was reading and following a book written by Dr. Spock. *Baby and Child Care* became her guide to childcare like it did for many mothers at the time.

Anyway, back to the delivery room. I began tracking my progress by what the doctor was wearing. First, he was in his street clothes, then partial scrubs, and finally full scrubs. He was an older gentleman and very old-school in his practices. When I asked him if Walter could come into the delivery room, he firmly said, "Absolutely not!" Then he said, "I don't want a second patient I need to revive after he faints."

His comment made me even more concerned. My mother had never told me what to expect during childbirth—the whole topic of sex education was never discussed. Therefore, I tried to prepare myself for what was ahead. I reassured myself that women had been giving birth since the dawn of time—it was part of the cycle of life. As my lower-back pain became intense and I could feel my baby shifting, I was finally wheeled into the delivery room.

After some instructions, and intense pushing, I felt a rush of warm liquid and relief.

"It's a girl," the doctor said as he made my daughter cry and handed her to the nurse. The nurse did the newborn care and wrapped her in a receiving blanket. My newborn baby was whisked away as the doctor cared for me.

I was devastated because I yearned to hold her, but all I saw was her tiny hand. I worried that something was wrong with her. She had barely cried—not at all like the cries I had heard from the other newborns.

When the doctor was finished, I was taken into the hallway. They didn't have a room ready for me, so I was in the hall for a while. Walter was sleeping around the corner in the waiting area. He finally came out to check on me and told me he had seen our precious daughter. "She is perfect," he said.

I was so exhausted that I fell asleep in the hall.

I was jarred awake when the bed began to move. We passed the nursery on the way to my room, but I couldn't see my daughter. Later that night, my long wait was finally over. A nun came in holding my daughter, wrapped in a blanket, and gently placed her in my arms. That was the first time I saw kindness in the nurse's eyes.

I uncovered my daughter's face and was filled with love for her. I gently let my fingers touch her soft, tiny face as I gazed into her beautiful, brown eyes. Her dark hair was so soft, like an angel's hair would be. In that moment, the cold world disappeared, and I was awed in so many ways.

Emma was perfect in every way. Ten fingers, ten toes, and everything any mother would wish for their child. From that day forth, I knew I would love her, treasure her, and cherish her for my entire life. I tenderly kissed her forehead and promised I would give her my eternal love. I promised I would always do my best to care for her, guide her, and teach her everything I could.

I had no idea Emma would be my saving grace. She was my reason to keep moving forward when life got ugly. I have experienced much, but the birth of my precious daughter will always be among my most treasured memories. A mother's love is unconditional and transcends all limits. No matter what happens, there is a special place in my heart for my daughter. Emma is my first child and my only daughter.

My Special Prayer

I am honored and truly blessed to be your mother.
From the moment I realized you were growing within me, I have cherished every minute of motherhood.
As I felt you moving and growing, I watched as my body changed and prepared for your special arrival.
Sometimes, in the early morning hours, I would softly speak to you as I watched the sunrise.
Other times, I would gently dance and sing to you.
It was a special time of youth and innocence.
I promised to do my best to care for you and teach you to be a strong, independent, and compassionate person.
On the day you were born, my heart overflowed with love as I cradled you, my precious daughter, in my arms.
I am truly humbled, even today, that your soul chose to honor me as your mother.
I tried to always teach you to listen to your small voice within.
The challenges of life can be bittersweet.
You have endured so much as you were growing up.

Sadly, you had to grow up too fast because of circumstances
out of your control.
Your life journey has been daunting at times, and through it all,
you have raised two outstanding sons.
Today, I understand we cannot teach what we have not learned.
We can only learn through our own life experiences.
At those most challenging times, we realize the answers we are
seeking have been inside us our whole life.
Listen to the small voice within you, for it will guide you to your
life purpose and unconditional love.
We have traveled many roads, through the years, some together
and others in different directions.
Time has been challenging as we have grown through
the ebb and flow of life.
The years have gone by quickly.
Always remember, my heart holds a special place for you.
I pray every evening that you will find what you are looking for.
May the True Source fill your heart and soul with peace and Love.

Buddha said, "How gently did you let go of things not meant
for you?"

What I have struggled with most is that our children are only our
responsibility for a few short years. In that time, we must nurture
them and teach them the skills to live a life of their own creation.
How they choose to live is up to them, and as parents, eventually,
we need to set them free and support them with unconditional love.
At that time, I was very codependent, and as my daughter grew, I
lacked the confidence to teach her self-reliance and independence.
Sadly, I was not the best role model. But I always honored my promise to love her and do my best to protect her.

Focus Questions

1. Are you a parent? Describe your life when you had your first child.

_____

_____

_____

_____

_____

_____

2. Describe how your parents felt about the birth of your first child.

_____

_____

_____

_____

_____

_____

3. Describe the type of parent or grandparent you are.

_____

_____

_____

_____

_____

_____

4. Describe the type of role model you are to your children.

_____

_____

_____

_____

_____

_____

Summary

Love and loyalty can be a double-edged sword. We always try to do our best for our children, despite what challenges we may be going through. Sometimes we have to make a difficult decision. As much as we may honor our family values and try to stay loyal to keeping a family together, people change. There comes a time when loyalty has to be relinquished for the love of our children.

Chapter 14

Living a Life Interrupted

Resilience

"Life can only be understood backwards,
it has to be lived forwards."

— Soren Kierkegaard

Walter, Emma, and I seemed to be settling into our new life until we were invaded. One night, I got up to feed the baby and went into the kitchen to warm her a bottle. When I opened the refrigerator door, I saw a large bug standing on the butter dish staring at me. I grabbed the baby bottle, slammed the door shut, and turned to the gas stove. When I turned the burner on, I heard crackling and saw more bugs on the other burners. I shrieked, and with Emma in my arms, I ran into the bedroom to tell Walter. He quickly checked the kitchen and came back to tell me we had cockroaches. I had never seen a cockroach, and I was ready to go sleep in the car. Walter calmed me down and said he would call the landlord in the morning.

I swaddled Emma and held her close to my bosom, sleeping with my infant daughter cradled in my arms and against my chest that night.

When the landlord arrived the next day, he told us he thought he had fumigated and gotten rid of the cockroaches, but when we talked, he realized the apartment had been vacant for a few weeks and the insects had gone to the apartment downstairs. Now that we had moved in, there was activity and food, which attracted the cockroaches. I became overly cautious with everything and insisted we find another apartment somewhere else. No way was I going to raise a toddler in this place.

We faced many stressors at the time. Prior to Emma's birth, Walter was seriously injured in an industrial accident. He worked as a sandblaster in a concrete casting company in Myerstown, Pennsylvania. The 3.5 ton casting was on a cart that moved along tracks through the plant, and it was Walter's job to sandblast the casting before it moved farther along the track. One day, the cart rolled off the tracks. The crane operator lifted the casting so Walter could lift the cart back onto the tracks. His hand was still on the cart when the casting was lowered back onto the cart and landed right on Walter's right thumb. Fortunately, Walter had just moved his fingers off the cart; however, his thumb was crushed, and a portion of his hand was badly injured. Through the next year, Walter underwent many reconstructive surgeries after the amputation of his thumb. One night, he got angry about what I served for dinner and began throwing things at me and attacking me. My fight or flight survival instincts kicked in, and I packed a diaper bag, picked up Emma and my wallet, and walked out into the cold, dark night. I had no idea where I was going, but I knew we needed to leave. We were not safe with Walter and the cockroaches.

I didn't know how to drive at the time. In fact, I was afraid to drive. So, I wrapped Emma in a blanket and walked to a park. Sitting on the bench, once again I thought about my options. Where could I go with a newborn, little money, no job, and no relatives? I was only twenty years old and did not know about any resources to help women in my position at that time. Once again, ignorance did not lead to bliss. The township was small and had no local police department. As the night air got cold, I thought I had only one option. Sadly, I took the slow, long walk back to the apartment. What I was learning was temperance—how to maintain self-control in a challenging situation.

The first year with Walter was an adjustment, as it is with many relationships. A newborn brings about more adjustments. With Walter's injuries, I chalked up his outbursts to his frustration, ongoing pain, and PTSD. Life is a collection of choices and events; some lead to blessings, others lead to more challenges. It is just the ebb and flow of life.

The town where we lived had few jobs, and with Walter's injury and limitations, we decided to move back to the West Coast. We headed to Yakima, Washington, for apple-picking season. This was a most excellent adventure. We had a 1972 Fiat Spider sports car. We added a large footlocker to the rack on the trunk and tucked our one-year-old daughter into the mini backseat. Life was finally turning a corner, and we were happy.

The industrial accident had cost Walter his right thumb, and when we headed for Yakima, his hand was still healing from the last of his many surgeries. Since our Fiat was a stick shift, I learned to shift gears based on the sound of the engine as Walter drove. I still did not have a driver's license, but together, we became a skilled driving duo. He operated the gas, clutch, and brakes, and I governed the gears.

Once we settled in Yakima, I decided it was time to try to reconcile with my parents. I had written to tell them they were grandparents when Emma was born, but we had not spoken in many months. I contacted them, and we arranged to meet in Seattle. Although in the beginning everyone felt awkward, a toddler is a great icebreaker. Relations remained distant for many years, but it was a beginning.

I also told them another grandchild was on the way. Family values are strong in our culture, and no matter what happens, the love for new family members is like the glue that reunites broken relationships. Rebuilding relationships takes time and understanding. Dealing with our emotions gave us an opportunity to put the past behind us. Everyone had made mistakes, and it was a time to move forward as a family.

Focus Questions

1. Describe some of your strong family values.

_____

_____

_____

_____

_____

_____

2. What are some of your family traditions? Do you follow them today?

_____

_____

_____

_____

_____

3. Describe your family life growing up.

_____

_____

_____

_____

_____

_____

4. Describe your communications with family today.

_____

_____

_____

_____

_____

_____

5. If family relationships are improving, how did reconciliation begin?

_____

_____

_____

_____

_____

Summary

When reconciling with loved ones who have hurt you, it's important to stay resilient. To rebuild communications takes patience and good listening skills. Everyone needs an opportunity to be heard and respected. Sometimes it only takes the effort to reconcile to begin the process. I remember dreading that talk with my father, but it never happened. When I tried to apologize, he took my daughter from my arms and just said, "It's water under the bridge." We never spoke about the "belt incident" again.

Chapter 15

Escalating Violence on the West Coast

Perseverance

"Being alone is scary, but not as scary as feeling alone in a relationship."

— Amelia Earhart

In the next five years, we moved about twelve times. Our son Roger was born in Oregon in 1975. It was a time of many blessings and challenges. Our family was blessed with a toddler and a newborn. With daycare costs rising, I was happy to be a stay-at-home mom. We really didn't have much, but I felt rich because I had my children.

Roger's birth was different than Emma's. We had a young obstetrician, who believed fathers should be in the delivery room. We planned for Walter to do so, but because too many births happened at the same time, fathers were left waiting in the labor rooms. It was still an improvement because Walter was able to support me through labor.

The small community hospital was busy that Memorial Day Weekend. I was in a labor room with another woman, and our husbands were with us. Walter and I had finally gotten married, and husbands were encouraged to help their wives through the labor process. Things were much different during this birth. But then each birth is unique. My doctor was a young man with red curls falling out from his cap. Even though this was my second birth, there were many little surprises. I remember as if it was yesterday, as I was in the final phase of pushing, the doctor said, "Stop!" His voice was firm, and I quickly stopped pushing. My baby's shoulder was stuck because he was turned to the side and the umbilical cord was wrapped around his neck. The doctor worked in silence and then he said, "Okay, now give one really big push." When I heard "It's a boy" and my son's first cries, I was relieved, and I was surprised when the doctor put him onto my stomach. But it was a little painful—my son weighed nine pounds. I was thrilled to be able to see him and touch his head. He wasn't left there long but truly a precious gift. I was completely thrilled that I had two children, one boy and one girl, and two happy arms to hold them both.

I knew my father would be excited to have a grandson in his family. No one to carry on the family name, but a boy nonetheless.

A funny side story was also unfolding. The nurse who was caring for me was positive that I would give birth to a girl, but I felt strongly it would be a boy. The nurse and I placed a bet. The prize was a triple-flavored popsicle. It was hot in Pendleton, Oregon, that day. When the doctor announced, I gave birth to my son, I squealed "I win!" The doctor was puzzled and just laughed it off. The nurse and I giggled a little and later that night, true to her word, she brought me a delicious, sweet popsicle. The cool treat was enjoyed but quickly forgotten when my son was placed into my arms for the first time.

My son has been such a blessing in my life from that day forward. His temperament has brought harmony and balance into my world. His easy-going attitude has enriched life in our home. As he grew, he would often bring his friends over, and at times, they would spend the night playing video games and eating us out of house and home. But back to when my beautiful children were young—there would be many times they would save my life. They gave me the reason to keep getting up and never giving up when life got ugly. As much as I tried to be a good role model, what I didn't realize was that I was codependent on my children.

We were thrilled to have a son and a daughter. Unfortunately, Walter couldn't keep a job, and a few months after Roger was born, we hit the road, traveling from Oregon back to Victoria and then to Las Vegas and several cities in Washington state as he tried to find gainful employment. We basically lived out of suitcases and boxes for six years.

Abuse was a family member during this time. Each event began to escalate from the previous one.

When our children were two and four, Walter worked in the prison system. We were struggling financially, as usual, so he kept encouraging me to get a job. Barely holding onto his own job, he spent his time looking through the newspapers for a job for me. But daycare costs were more than I could earn, and I wanted to be a stay-at-home mom, like my mother. My father believed the man in the family should be the breadwinner and the woman belonged at home caring for the family. Besides, our children were just coming into their own character, and I wanted to show them the beauty of the world.

We were living in Vancouver in a small one-bedroom apartment. Walter was relentlessly urging me to become an exotic dancer. He knew how I loved to dance, but I had no intention of compromising my ethics. Walter continued to badger me because exotic dancers earned a good income. Walter's abusive behavior followed him to work and escalated to the point where he was suspended from his job. He was warned that if he did not attend anger management counseling, he would be fired. With Walter's suspension, I was forced to accept a job Walter arranged for me with a nightclub owner. I knew I had to provide food and shelter for the children, so I became an exotic dancer. The position compromised my moral code, but I knew I would get paid every night. The money I earned in tips was used to buy food for the children and the weekly pay was used for bills.

The job required costumes, fittings, music, and stage production. Everything was new to me, but I made a couple of friends who helped me adjust and gave me tips on how to keep my distance from questionable customers. We had bouncers protecting us as well. This was truly a different world. I had never dreamt I would do this, but I ended up doing it for a year. The only saving grace was that, between the contract and daily tips, I was able to feed my children.

I soon noticed Walter lurking in the shadows at the back of the nightclub when I was working. One night, I approached him to ask who was watching the children and what was he doing there. His answer was vague. He implied a neighbor was checking in on the children. He would leave when I went back to the dressing room. He would be home before I got back, so I never knew who was watching my children. Writing this, I wonder if he had left the children alone because they were sleeping. The more he came to the nightclub, the more jealous he became. He accused me of cheating on him. The abuse escalated into physical violence. I was forced to create ways to hide my many bruises to keep my job.

One night when I was home especially stands out as being traumatic. Walter had been drinking most of the day, and he started an argument. I could see the warning signs—this would be a bad one. I gathered books and toys and hid the children in the closet with flashlights. I told them to be quiet and play. Emma loved her books, and Roger had his favorite cars and toys. I told the children, "No matter what you hear, stay in the closet. I will come get you as soon as I can."

Walter was enraged, angry over some imaginary infidelity or other offense he thought I had committed. The moment I closed the closet door, he stepped into the bedroom, picked me up, and threw me against the side of the bed on my stomach. I grabbed a pillow, knowing I had to stay quiet. I will spare you the details, but that night I learned what spousal rape truly felt like. My face was buried deeply in the pillow as I muffled my crying, enduring the most heartbreaking pain. I felt more than just physical pain; the emotional pain was devastating.

When Walter finished beating me, he stormed out of the room, got a beer out of the refrigerator, and walked out of the apartment. I pulled myself together, wiped away my tears, and opened the closet door. The children were still quietly playing, and I sat in the closet with them, just hugging them. Feeling alone with two small children tore my heart apart.

My memory of this traumatic event became the ever-growing inner parasite that would devour my caring spirit. It shredded pieces of my soul, and I buried the experience deeply, never to be shared until now.

Years have passed since it happened. Although I swore to myself I would never share this story, I know there are people going through similar experiences right now. I can quote statistics, but that is not why I am sharing my stories. Somewhere in the world, right now, someone is feeling the hands of their abuser choking their last breath of life out of their lungs. Someone else is feeling the pain of their skin being ripped apart through sexual abuse and praying that they will just die. Someone else is searching for a way to escape their abuser; they are running into a dark, cold forest, barefoot and wearing nothing more than torn shorts and a tank top.

Abuse and domestic violence are often ignored and swept aside. Yet they are so prevalent. Victims stay with or return to their abusers because they are afraid to leave or do not know they have choices. Victims stay for many reasons like lack of money or limited beds at the shelters.

People in desperate situations often become statistics because no one knows they are desperately in need of help. Victims feel like they have no place to go. Abusers create so much fear in their victims that the victims are silenced.

No one knew what had happened to me, and worse, I didn't believe anyone cared or would help even if they did know.

A few days later, Walter returned to work. We soon moved to another city, closer to his work. I was happy to leave the world of exotic dancing. Christmas was approaching, and I just wanted to enjoy the holidays in our new home. The children were three and five, and we needed to settle down somewhere because Emma would be starting school soon.

Our constant moves were becoming more difficult for the children. Everything was always new, and we had no friends, childcare help, or family around. Walter continued to struggle with keeping a job, and he became even more violent.

Walter wanted me to go back to exotic dancing, but I refused. One night, in a rage, he threw a box of old family Christmas decorations on the floor. Then he crushed each precious ornament from my grandmother under his feet. The decorations were family heirlooms. When I tried to stop him, he threw a coffee table at me. I ducked just in time, but I could not dodge the assault that came next. As I ran into the kitchen, he grabbed my arm and began smashing my head into the kitchen cabinets and walls. I'm glad the children were upstairs.

Someone must have heard the noise. As the police sirens got closer, Walter charged out of the townhouse, grabbing the car keys. I tried to stop him from driving away in that state of mind, but he went.

Walter did not get far. He put the car in the ditch across the road. The police were on the scene within minutes.

I am sure people wonder why I didn't just take the children and leave. At times, I wonder that myself. Why did I endure so many years of abuse? My answer is simple: I convinced myself it was not that bad. It wasn't his fault. He had PTSD. I came up with many reasons to stay. After learning about other victims of domestic violence, I compared my injuries and stories to theirs and thought, *My injuries aren't that bad!*

In reality, *no one should ever abuse another person*. No matter how minor the injury or abuse is—**it is not okay. Do not accept it or stay with your abuser!**

But at that time, I felt helpless. I had no family in the country. My work experience and skills were only enough to earn minimum wage and not enough to pay for childcare. Let me be clear. I had options, but like most victims of domestic abuse, I was scared, alone, and felt like I had no choice, no escape.

Why did I stay? Codependence? I knew it was a toxic relationship, but I didn't know what to do. While researching behaviors for this book, I learned the term "trauma bond." Licensed clinical social worker (LCSW) Sherry Gaba wrote, "Trauma bonding is similar to Stockholm Syndrome, in which people held captive come to have feelings of trust or even affection for the very people who captured and held them against their will."

The codependent feels loved and cared for, but as the relationship erodes, the emotional, mental, and physical abuse escalates. Gaba writes in *Wake Up Recovery*, "The more the codependent reaches out to the narcissist for love, recognition, and approval, the more the trauma bond is strengthened." When the codependent stays in the relationship, the escalating abuse creates a destructive cycle. Separation, acknowledging one's own choices, and developing a support network are required strategies to assist the codependent in separating from the destructive relationship.

Focus Questions

1. When forced to decide, how do you choose between two bad options?

_____

_____

_____

_____

_____

_____

2. Describe a moment when you felt defeated.

_____

_____

_____

_____

_____

_____

3. Describe any family support you had during these challenging times.

_____

_____

_____

_____

_____

_____

4. Why did you make the choices you did?

_____

_____

_____

_____

_____

_____

Summary

In challenging relationships, it is easy to find yourself facing decisions between two evils. You really don't want to choose either option, but you know something needs to be done. It takes perseverance to stay strong during these times. I always chose what I believed would be the best for the children. During these times of abuse, I did not reach out to family. I didn't want to hear my father's lecture, and most of the time, we lived too far away from my parents. What I have since learned is that parents can offer comfort, advice, and options we may not have thought about. Reach out and let them know what is happening to you.

Chapter 16

Teaching the Children

Self-Reliance

"Family is the most important thing in the world."

— Princess Diana

One of the most inspirational women in history, Princess Diana, showed so much integrity and compassion throughout her life. After she married Prince Charles, the eldest son of Queen Elizabeth II, in 1981, she took on many duties on behalf of the queen. Although the royal marriage ended in divorce in 1996, she continued to raise awareness for AIDS and campaign for the removal of landmines. The media praised her for her unconventional approach to working with charities. Her earlier work was focused on children and youth, but it spread to many diverse causes.

While Princess Diana worked diligently to help in areas many considered dangerous, she continued to raise her sons by showing them a lifestyle many young royals had been denied. Although very protective of her sons, William and Harry, she broke royal protocol, and the young family enjoyed skiing and amusement parks.

When Princess Diana married Prince Charles, I could see her shyness radiating through the TV coverage of their wedding. I admired her self-control, even though I could sense her insecurities over the life she was beginning. At the time, I felt very timid and insecure. As Diana's marriage began to blossom, or so we were led to believe, my marriage was falling apart. While tabloids reported rumors that Prince Charles was having an affair with Camilla Parker Bowles, my abusive husband was having extramarital affairs.

I was thrilled when the royal couple had a son, and then a second son—"an heir and a spare." As I followed Princess Diana's story, in some ways, I think I was living vicariously through her. Sadly, although both of us believed family was the most important thing in the world, our husbands did not consider family the top priority. At least she was married to a future king. I was married to an unemployed, lazy, alcoholic with a gambling addiction.

One of the most difficult things mothers endure is working away from home. Children are often sent to daycare or babysitters. When my children were young, I was desperately trying to survive each day. My main concern was providing food, clothing, and a home for my children. My heart ached desperately when I left my children with the elderly woman who lived across from the hospital where I worked night shift.

Although it was an exhausting time, it was peaceful because my abusive husband Walter was working out of town. I didn't see the money he supposedly earned, but perhaps we received token payments. Unfortunately, the quality of time I had with my children was poor because I took them to the sitter after dinner and only slept three hours before I went to work. After working all night as a certified nurse's aide (CNA), I forced myself to stay awake to care for my children.

That schedule did not work for long. I became a walking zombie. Emma and Roger were five and three, and they helped as much as their little hands could. I fell asleep on the couch one extremely exhausting day and woke to the sound of running water in the kitchen. I went to check on the noise and found my five-year-old daughter standing on a chair washing dishes and my three-year old son drying them with a towel. Roger apologized for not being able to put the dishes into the cupboard—he was too small to reach the shelf. Emma had washed the dishes in cold water.

All I could do was hug them both.

I had not yet realized that children truly learn by watching what adults do. This was a beautiful story of how they were watching and learning. They tried to help as much as they could so I could sleep a little. Emma and Roger were very responsible at their young ages.

Often, one of the children would come out from playing quietly in the bedroom and cover me with a blanket. We lived in a tiny apartment, and I slept by the front door so I could hear if they went outside.

Whether we raise our children in an affluent or a low-income home, love matters most. When children live in a home where abuse in any form is evident, they grow up believing abusive behaviors are normal. They have nothing to compare their lives to. These learned behaviors stay with the children long into adulthood unless the cycle is broken. Children raised in abusive homes continue the pattern as adults. Even if as adults they realize their situation is abusive, they feel comfortable because it is what they are used to—it is their comfort zone.

They often overlook, for many reasons, the reality that a better life exists just outside their comfort zone. Some are afraid to break the cycle because it feels strange, and they do not feel worthy of a life of respect, love, and abundance. Victims often lack confidence and are afraid to face the world on their own. All the demeaning and insulting comments often take away any shred of independence a person may have had. Some victims have become so brainwashed that they do not consider seeking resources that could help them.

There are six different types of abuse, and many of them are brought into our lives in subtle ways: physical, sexual, verbal/emotional, mental/psychological, financial, and cultural. I had experienced the physical and sexual many times. But I didn't realize that I was brainwashed. It would be years before I realized the depth of the mental abuse I endured.

"The most difficult thing is the decision to act,
the rest is merely tenacity.
The fears are paper tigers.
You can do anything you decide to do.
You can act to change and control your life,
and the procedure, the process is its own reward."

— Amelia Earhart

As I have heard many times, "Life is not a dress rehearsal." We all have one chance to live our lives and reach our greatest potential. The problem is many people are just like I was—sacrificing themselves for the benefit of others because we love them. That is a noble task, to be sure, but at what cost? We spill blood, sweat, and tears for our children and aging parents, and we justify our actions as love.

But often, our compassion, understanding, and loving empathy are not returned, leaving us feeling used and empty. As mentioned earlier, our soul is remembering and learning through our experiences. It makes us who we are. We are all an aspect of God, the True Source, and we are created from unconditional love. Being of love and giving love to others is what we all do. But so often, we become too busy simply surviving, and we forget to love the most important person in our lives—*ourselves!*

When I first heard this concept, I felt like it was arrogant. In my list of priorities, I had placed my needs after the needs of everyone else I loved. That is a mistake many of us make. We cannot teach what we do not know, just as we cannot pour from an empty cup. It is imperative we practice self-care so we will always have an abundant heart capable of serving to enrich the lives of others.

I share my life journey—from the swill under the gutter to the beautiful, overwhelming feeling of unconditional love—because I have finally learned to accept who I am. When you begin to connect with and understand your true self, you discover your soul and the beautiful, loving person you truly are. Everyone has a story, and it really does not matter where you come from. What matters is that you are perfect within yourself right now. When you begin to love yourself, you grow ever more perfect, and you radiate loving energy from within out to the world and the people around you. People will be drawn to you because your energy is positive—nothing negative can survive in positivity.

Just Be You—Just Love You—Just Trust You

It is easy to say to just be you, but it is one of the most challenging things to do. We are so focused on being successful and providing for others that we have little time left to focus on our own needs. To begin healing your heartaches, you must bring them out of hiding and honestly look at them for what they are.

Take responsibility for *only* your part, not the whole thing. Look at heartaches, understand them, and then release that painful energy. It is important to love yourself, and those who have hurt you, and most importantly, to forgive yourself! It is time to learn who you really are, recognize your passion, and discover your mission and goals. The memories will always be with you, but they will only be a reminder of what you endured—and that you are better for the experience. Hold onto the lesson; let the heartache go.

Remember, through the course of our lives, our soul feels all our emotions. Our soul, also known as our higher self, knows what we have been through. Every time we were abused, betrayed, got bullied, or endured negative comments, a piece of our soul was torn away and went into hiding somewhere deep within our core. As we grow up, those pieces of our soul remain hidden. Our self-worth, self-love, and self-esteem continue to diminish. But we continue to function because our family depends on us. Over time, more of our soul tears away, and we become bitter and driven by ego. We may try to soothe our feelings with material things—new cars, fancy homes, clothes, and luxurious trips. The reality is that those things are a vain search for our sense of personal value. The caveat is we cannot take possessions with us when we depart this life. The only thing of value we can take with us is unconditional love, which brings me back to my point.

When you are being abused, your soul is being torn with every insult, negative action, physical injury, or criticism. Those pieces of your soul go into hiding deep within your core. As you continue to struggle with stress and challenges, those negative energies are like a parasite that eats away at your body and can manifest as physical illnesses, aches, and pains—even panic attacks. As a survivor of long-term domestic violence and abuse, I had no idea how to handle stress. Alcohol became my friend, my crutch when I was afraid to go home.

When we lived in Walla Walla, Washington, Walter still couldn't keep a job, so I decided to get a government job. Walter told me they wouldn't hire me, but I took the four-hour test anyway. When I passed with a 96 percent score, I was elated, and the world around me began to change. However, I was disappointed, though I understood, when the job was given to a veteran.

Life was challenging. Walter got a job near Everett, Washington. Once again, we packed up the children and moved to a different one-bedroom apartment. I watched for job vacancies where my test scores would help me get hired. My scores were transferred to an office in Snohomish, Washington. They had three vacancies, so I went to talk to the manager every day, trying to secure one of the jobs. On my third visit, when I knocked on the office door—in my mind the door looked ten feet tall and it seemed the manager loomed in the doorway like Goliath—the manager opened the door and stared down at me. I kept my focus.

I met with the manager and his assistant manager. I was questioned relentlessly, but I had answers for everything. I desperately needed the job because I knew it was only a matter of time before Walter would be jobless again. After a battery of questions, the two men looked at each other, and then the assistant manager suggested they should give me a chance.

I was thrilled. I would finally have a job—it was only one day a week, but I was also a substitute when needed. It did not sound like much of a job, and it was hard work, but I knew I had my foot in the door with a government job. My goal was to work it into a fulltime job. That would take time, but for the first time, I felt like I could finally breathe, knowing we would have food on the table for our growing children.

When Walter heard that I finally got a good job, he quit his. I was devastated because, once again, our financial security was in question. I kept our family going with one full-time job and two part-time jobs. All the while, I still lived with my unemployed husband. I watched as he destroyed our finances while refusing even to apply for unemployment benefits. His only responsibility was to take care of the children. He drank alcohol all day long, and when the children were in school, he entertained himself with the neighbor's wife and other women.

Living with Walter was like walking on eggshells because I never knew what mood he would be in when I returned from my ten- to fourteen-hour workdays.

I often stood in line at the foodbank to get powdered milk, cheese, and potatoes. All my paychecks together kept us just at the poverty line. I did not qualify for welfare because I was working and our income was barely over the limits, but we did qualify for the foodbank.

After a year and a half juggling three jobs, I found an opportunity for a full-time government job in Winslow, Washington. I had no idea where it was at the time, but I applied for the position because I would be able to quit the part-time jobs. The location was remote, so it was not a job anyone else wanted.

When I got the job, it was my first full-time job with the government. I was thrilled because we finally had a regular paycheck and medical insurance. Once again, we packed up and relocated, but this time, I knew we could finally unpack and put down roots in our new community.

We relocated in 1983, but this time, the move was because I was in control and had secured a full-time position with the government. After years of financial insecurity, we finally had stability and medical insurance. I was thrilled when I was able to buy a decent car and a mobile home.

Walter had been unemployed for several years, and he refused to apply for benefits because that meant he had to look for work. Since my workday didn't end until that day's influx was complete, I went home at varying times. When I knew Walter would probably be upset, I stopped for a drink on the way home. Jack Daniels was my liquid courage. Sadly, this pattern continued for many years.

Focus Questions

1. Describe a time you had to take control of your life.

_____

_____

_____

_____

_____

_____

2. Describe a time you were caught up in an addiction.

_____

_____

_____

_____

_____

_____

3. Describe the situation and what you did to handle it.

_____

_____

_____

_____

_____

_____

4. What was the outcome?

_____

_____

_____

_____

_____

Summary

Family is always a valued priority, but we must also become self-reliant to provide the best of us to our family. It is important to recognize our strengths and weaknesses in order to build ourselves into confident role models for our children. If we are codependent or lack self-worth, self-love, and self-esteem, we are not setting strong examples for our children. It's important to assess your own personal learned behavior. Then ask yourself, "What am I teaching my children? Am I a good example?"

Chapter 17

Awakening the Silent Warrior

Courage

"I learned that courage was not the absence of fear,
but the triumph over it."

— Nelson Mandela

By 1986, Walter had been unemployed for three years. Life had been getting progressively worse, and I was tired of being the only responsible adult. I felt like I had three children. Then, on the night of July 4, everything changed.

We were at a neighbor's birthday party and Fourth of July celebration. All the children were upstairs playing. The place was packed with people. There was lots of music and delicious food, and everyone had brought their own alcohol. A friend was showing off his motorcycle and offered to take me for a ride. I checked with Walter; he asked me to stop at our house and bring more beer. I liked motorcycles. I jumped on, and we enjoyed a beautiful summer night ride.

We stopped at the house for the beer and returned to the party. I did not think we had been gone long, but we had talked some at the house. Walter felt we had been gone too long, enough time for me to cheat on him.

The argument began the moment I gave him the beer. Fortunately, I got him outside to our truck, away from the happy people partying. There was no need to ruin the party for the others. Walter was screaming and pushing me, and as soon as he unlocked the truck, he grabbed me by the shoulders and threw me onto the seat. He slapped and punched me as I tried to slide over to the passenger door.

Before I could get out the other door, he had his hands around my neck, and he was slamming my head against the inside of the passenger window. I prayed I would pass out. But he kept slamming my head against the window while yelling and choking me.

I looked up through my tears and could see my children from the light in the bedroom. They were looking out the window. To this day, I do not know if they saw what was happening, but I vividly remember something inside me snapping. At that moment, my mindset shifted; I fought back like a warrior. I used every part of my body to get him off me so I could to pry his fingers off my neck. With every fiber of my strength, I twisted his hands and pushed with all my might to get out of the truck. The passenger door was locked, but I somehow managed to unlock it, jump out, and run into the house.

I just kept thinking, *This is my Independence Day*. In that moment, I promised myself no one would ever hurt me again!

In the house, I hurried to find my girlfriend and quickly asked her if the kids could spend the night. I told her it was not safe for them to come home with us. She asked if I was all right. I shook my head, but I told her I had to be okay. I could see Walter watching me, and I excused myself. She told me I could come back and spend the night if need be.

Walter left as I went upstairs to say goodnight to my children. He had already driven to the house. I think I walked home, but I do not remember. He did not have his house key, so when I arrived at the house, I found him sleeping in an old delivery van we owned. Something came over me, perhaps my silent warrior, when I saw him passed out on the floor of the van. I quietly opened the back door and did something out of character.

Under the cover of night, with only one streetlight, I grabbed Walter's head and started pounding it into the floor of the van. In my tears and rage, I remember thinking, *This is what it feels like when you pound my head into the wall. I hope you feel this when you wake up.* I had no concept of time. Walter never woke up, and I quietly stepped out of the van and closed the door.

Everything changed that night.

I locked him out of the house and tried to figure out what I should do. As I paced back and forth, I thought back to previous incidents when I had called the local police, but they were no help. My bruises always appeared the next day. After repeated police visits with no results, I gave up on getting help from law enforcement. I was afraid to stay at the house because of what Walter had already done. I could feel the lumps swelling on the back of my head, and I knew I needed to find a safe place for the night.

I grabbed a jacket, my purse, a couple of cans of beer, and jumped into my car. Totally the wrong thing to do, but I was operating in survival mode and seeking a safe place to go. I had no family or close friends, and the only safe place I could go was our local fire hall. I knew the fire chief only a little, but in my moment of helplessness, it was the only place I could find refuge from my abuser.

When I got to the firehall, a few miles from my house, only a few people were inside. I parked my car haphazardly, turned it off, and cried. Again, I had no concept of time. I just cried and trembled. When the firefighters came to my car, they asked me to open the window. I was so afraid. I made sure my doors were locked. After much effort, they finally convinced me to open my window a crack so they could talk to me. I cried so hard that I could not breathe and could barely talk. I just shook my head as the tears kept rolling down my face. When they asked if I was all right, I just shook my head. They asked me if I wanted to go inside. I refused. They saw the beer cans and told me if I drove away, I would be arrested for driving under the influence. I thought, *I have nowhere to go*.

One kind firefighter asked if I wanted to talk to the fire chief. I just cried, nodded my head, and put my face in my hands. When the fire chief arrived and I heard his gentle voice, I looked up. He was the only one I knew there. He asked if I would like to come inside and have some coffee to warm up a little. After a little coaxing, I finally agreed. I gave my car keys to a firefighter, who moved my car as the fire chief wrapped a blanket around my shoulders and walked me into the firehouse.

After some warm coffee and kind words, I was finally able to share my story. It was the beginning of a long road to recovery. I will always have the scars and three dented spots on the back of my skull. The fire chief asked if I wanted to press charges against Walter. I was too afraid to do anything at that time. So as daylight broke, the fire chief gave me some information on what I needed to do and the resources available to me. I am eternally grateful that he came to my rescue that early morning.

It was time for me to leave the firehouse's safety. I gathered my thoughts and was glad to see the beer had been removed from my car, and I was legal to drive again. It was too early to pick up the children, so I went back to the house. Walter was sitting in his truck, smoking a cigarette. When I walked past him, he tried to apologize. All I could do was walk into the bathroom, lock the door, and sit on the floor. It was the only safe place I had in the house. I knew this would be the honeymoon period, and he would apologize until another cycle of violence began.

The movie *The Burning Bed* came out that year. In it, the wife sets fire to the bedroom in a desperate effort to end the abuse she is suffering. I could relate to how desperately she wanted the abuse to end.

Years earlier, despite my abuser's negative comments, I had bought a double-wide mobile home. We lived in it as a family for about three years. When I reached my limit with Walter's abuse, I knew I could no longer keep living like that. After serious consideration, I purchased a gas can, filled it, and researched how long it would take to destroy a mobile home. I secured the full gas can in my trunk and waited for the opportunity, when Walter was passed out, to tuck the children into the backseat of the car under blankets and set the mobile home on fire. Everything I treasured in the material world was inside, but I treasured a better life for the three of us. I was determined to do it if I had to. Thankfully, I never did.

The next few months were a rollercoaster of emotions. I counted my blessings that Walter finally had a job out of town and was only home a couple of nights a week. I began seeing a counselor, and I took Emma and Roger with me, hoping they could also have some-one to talk to. It was clearly a difficult time for all of us. They were thirteen and eleven now but did not really know what was happen-ing to our family.

I finally worked up the courage to kick Walter's abusive ass out. My counselor taught me, when Walter asked to come home, that if I could not say "no" to just say "maybe." So that is how my new life would begin. On a hope, many prayers, and occasional "maybes."

Walter did not like this change in my behavior and began stalk-ing me. I soon learned he had lost his job again. He could never hold a job for more than a few months at best.

One night, Walter called, begging me to let him come home. As I sat on the floor in the bathroom, with my back against the door, I was surprised to hear a loud "F..K NO!" explode from my lips. For the first time in my married life, I had finally spoken my mind and refused to compromise. He begged. I said no and hung up the phone.

The Games People Play

Pretty soon, Walter started playing mind games. Fortunately, I was working with a counselor at the time. Sometimes, I drove up to my mailbox after a long day at work only to be surprised by Walter jumping at me from behind the bushes. It startled me. Walter's be-havior put me in an awkward situation because I knew he wanted to see the children. They needed to see their father, too, but when I would concede and allow him to visit the kids, he spent the whole time trying to get us back together. When I encouraged him to spend time with the children, he said he really had no idea what to do with them. I told him just to talk to them, encourage them, and for heaven's sake, just love them.

Walter's visits became too stressful for everyone, so after a few attempts, I refused to let him visit. Then the constant phone calls began. He called late at night to tell me he was going to kill himself. He had no job and was living in a motel in the city. He was running out of money and contemplating jumping out of a fourth-floor window. His voice was pleading, and it tore at my heart. I could not take the chance of physically going to help him. In desperation, at 2:00 a.m., I called my counselor. To this day, I am so grateful he answered the phone and helped me through that night.

I refused to drive to the city to rescue Walter. Instead, I stayed home with the children. What I did do was…give him hope. Christmas was only a few days away, and I told Walter he could come spend Christmas with us. The children would like to see him, and I would be off work so we could be together one last time. After several months of counseling, I knew this would be our last family Christmas together, and I knew I was strong enough to recognize the games he was playing with me. I set the rules and warned Walter that the minute he bent or broke them, he would have to leave. He agreed, and I shared the news with Emma and Roger. They were glad to hear Walter was coming, but they were a bit apprehensive because their last visit with their dad had been a disaster.

Christmas Day 1986 was bittersweet. We worked to make the day special, with gifts, a tree, decorations, and a wonderful meal. It was a nice, peaceful day, filled with laughter, stories, and a few movies. I saw the joy in my children's eyes and felt terrible knowing it would probably be their last Christmas with their father. I had already decided the marriage was over. But that was not something I wanted to tell the children on Christmas Day. So, I stored that information away in my heart as I watched them enjoy the time together.

When the evening was over and Emma and Roger headed for bed, I tucked them in and told them how much I loved them, knowing all the while that the following day I would be telling them their father and I were separating. I did not have the heart to say the word divorce, even though I knew that was my next step.

Walter was going to spend the night on the couch, and as I found a pillow and blanket for him, I thought about our life together. I remembered our chance meeting in Hawaii, how he had traveled from Oahu to Canada to find me, and the way we had found each other at Niagara Falls. I thought of all the times our paths could have diverged, sending us in different directions, yet we kept finding each other. Was it all divine intervention?

Today, I understand that our souls had agreed to meet in this lifetime so they could learn through our life experiences. But I did not know that back in 1986. I just followed my heart.

Walter was sitting alone on the couch when I came into the living room with the bedding. He was looking at the pictures on the walls around the room. He was a very broken man. I walked over and invited him to join me in the bedroom.

Yes, that house held many painful memories, but on that Christmas night, I wanted to bring a gentle memory into both of our lives. Neither one of us knew what our future held. I knew there had been good times in our past. Our lives came together for a reason, but we struggled for years to find our way. Yes, Walter had PTSD, and yes, I struggled with intense codependency, but I believe there is good in everyone.

Behind closed doors, we remembered the love we had had for each other. It was a special night in the arms of love and amazing grace. I had already decided to end the marriage. This was our last night together. Our lives would never return to these few beautiful hours together. Yes, there were difficult times between us, and we had many lessons to learn, but for one moment, *love* prevailed. I have never regretted this decision.

The next morning, when it was time for Walter to leave, we talked to the children together and separately with each one. Emma was distant with me, and Roger was crushed and upset. I will never forget his words, "You promised me you would stay together and work it out!" Those words broke my heart.

Emma and Roger said goodbye to Walter and disappeared into their bedrooms. I walked Walter out to his truck and watched him drive away. I wanted to be sure he got on the ferry to the mainland, so I jumped into my car and followed him from a distance. I parked on a hillside and watched as he drove his truck onto the ferry. I felt a burden was lifted and slowly drove home.

I parked my car. Then the reality began to flow through me. I was finally alone! How would I survive and provide for my children? I went inside and closed the front door. I leaned against the rigid wood and slid to the floor in a flood of tears. Thankfully, Emma and Roger were still in their bedrooms and did not hear me come in. I sat there in the entryway with my arms wrapped around my knees and tears flowing down my cheeks. I trembled. It felt like I had an enormous hole in my soul—large enough to drive a semi-truck through.

When I heard Emma and Roger coming out of their bedrooms, I wiped away my tears, got off the floor, and went over to comfort them. They were young, and now I was their only parent. During the next few months, I struggled with panic attacks, feelings of insecurity, and how I would provide for my family. It was truly a memorable, bittersweet Christmas.

Focus Questions

1. Think of a painful moment. What part did you play that led up to that moment?

_____

_____

_____

_____

_____

_____

2. Was it a case of miscommunication? Describe.

_____

_____

_____

_____

_____

_____

3. What other actions could you have taken?

_____

_____

_____

_____

_____

_____

4. How did you decide to take control?

_____

_____

_____

_____

_____

Summary

We hear that courage is just beyond fear. What we often forget to look at is the courageous acts we perform. It's easy to give opinions and advice, but when it's you against your fears, will you deeply inhale and forge forward into the unknown? As much as I tried to be a good role model, what I didn't realize was I was codependent with my children. I didn't adapt well to being a single parent. Sadly, I held onto them too tightly and lacked the ability to teach them some of the life skills they would require. But we can't teach something we don't know, so we all learned in our own way. When you face your fears, you will find your courage to keep going forward. Just remember that everyone has their own life journey; let your children have theirs too.

Part III

Searching for My Purpose

Chapter 18

Introduction to Finding Purpose in My Life

Hospitality/Generosity

"Do what you feel in your heart to be right—
for you'll be criticized anyway.
You'll be damned if you do, and damned if you don't."

— Eleanor Roosevelt

One of the most difficult things to recognize is the masks people wear. Most of my life, I thought people were as loving, trusting, and empathetic as I am. When I was a teenager, my mother told me I had an old soul. Back then, I could not really understand what she meant. Decades later, I have learned many lessons the hard way. People are not always whom they appear to be, and many are nothing like me at all! I have always been quick to love, trust, and forgive when others have hurt me. For most of my life, I would say, "I have a long cord to a nasty temper," but most people have never seen my silent warrior side! Perhaps it comes from my Viking ancestry! It has always been my goal to help others less fortunate than me. I have tried to do that in different ways. At times, I had to face my fears to step out of my comfort zone to help others.

"Our deepest fear is not that we are inadequate.
Our deepest fear is that we are powerful beyond measure."

— Marianne Williamson

It was nice when the holiday season ended and my children were able to return to school. Through the difficult holiday, while I had to return to work, I had my children spending time with friends, and I was grateful they were able to be part of healthy family celebrations. Once school began and life took a new direction, I continued with the bowling league I was in. So many things were revealed to me by some of the other league members. I began to realize Walter had been taking money out of the league account while I was a treasurer for it. I tried to replace the money, so I was devastated when my credibility was destroyed and I had to face some serious investigations.

For my children's sake, I tried to keep a normal routine, even though I just wanted to gather my thoughts and start planning a different life for my children. During one of these awkward times on the bowling league, I noticed a man constantly watching me. Here, at the most vulnerable point in my life, I became prey to another narcissist! Little did I know he was setting me up as his next victim. Naïve me fell for this guy who promised me everything and delivered more of the same garbage I had just stepped away from. The only difference was this man did not raise a hand to hurt me, but he still destroyed the little self-worth I had left. Once again, I got reeled in like a sucker fish! I was only trying to help someone less fortunate than I was.

At this point, I had barely begun to stand on my own two feet, and I did not have the confidence to say "No" to anyone. I desperately wanted to feel like I belonged. Before long, my codependent behaviors kicked in again. Now I thought I had someone in my life who made me feel like I mattered. This entire mindset had begun when I was just four and had almost drowned. No one knew how small I felt and how scared I was.

My father had been my hero because he was strong, and at times, he did spend time with me. In fact, when I was little, I learned to dance the polka and the waltz with my papa. I would stand on his feet and he would hold my hands as we danced in circles around the basement to old Estonian music. My father had hoped he would have a son, so he was a bit disappointed when I was born. I was a tomboy who always tried to be the son he desired. I would go fishing with him and my grandfather, but my father always treated me like a bit of a helpless girl. When it came to putting the worm on the hook, he never let me try to do it myself. I chuckle now because, in his own way, he was protecting me as his little girl. In retrospect, I think I was still looking for a man like my father who would take care of me and make me feel safe.

When the new man, George, entered my life, I thought my struggles would be over. He was someone I thought would be my partner and help me with the challenges of being a single mom. He was living with his brother because he couldn't support himself. That should have been a red flag for me, but once again, I was trusting and afraid. One night when he came over to my house, carrying an armload of pizza, my kids were in heaven, and before I realized it, he was living rent-free in my house. The trade-off, in my eyes, was that he was taking care of my children when I was working; it gave me comfort to know my children were no longer latch-key kids. But, once again, at what cost did I sacrifice my time with my children? Time was already scant because they were becoming teenagers and I spent so much time working, so I was not there for them.

It took six years and a few other people to show me that once again I was being used. While Walter had not used me in the beginning—or perhaps he did and I was just naïve—I definitely saw how I was used by George. I have always been very trusting, which I believe has been my downfall. I have always been quick to give love and trust, which has set me up for challenging life events and financial losses. But my greatest loss will always be the time I worked so much, consequently denying myself that time with my greatest loves of all, my children.

Ironically, both of my exes ended up being long-haul truck drivers. When I learned of more infidelity in my life, I got angry, and despite my fear of driving long distances, I drove to Salt Lake City on a whim and a prayer. I knew George was in a relationship with a woman in Salt Lake City. She was half my age, and he wanted a child. I knew having a child was important to him, and I could no longer have children. I drove to the truck stop in Salt Lake City to warn her about his manipulative behaviors and let her know she could keep him. I took back to her some of her belongings that George had. I had reached a point of being done! I no longer wanted to play games. In Salt Lake City, I met her for coffee and gave her the belongings and my prayers. As we sat in the coffee shop, George walked in and said, "Outside now. I want to talk to you." I politely told him I would meet him in the parking lot when I was done talking to his new friend. He stormed out of the coffee shop. That was one of my first actions to empower myself and take control of my life.

When I was done talking to George's friend, I paid my bill and calmly walked out to my car. George was leaning on a railing smoking a cigarette and fuming. My message was simple. He was no longer welcome in my home, and he had two weeks to get his property out of my yard.

Again, he tried to play games with me. He even tried to use my children as tools to get to me. But I stood strong in my belief that I no longer needed anyone in my life. I was finally beginning to break my codependent thinking.

Focus Questions

1. Do you remember a time when you felt someone was using you? Describe how you felt.

_____

_____

_____

_____

_____

_____

2. Describe how you handled that situation.

_____

_____

_____

_____

_____

3. What were the results?

_____

_____

_____

_____

_____

_____

4. Were children involved? Were the children used as pawns?

_____

_____

_____

_____

_____

_____

Summary

Being hospitable and generous are excellent characteristics. However, some individuals see those traits as an invitation for them to prey on you. Be mindful of those who present themselves one way, but lack credibility. Giving them a hand only enables them to continue their toxic behavior. Teaching them how to lift themselves up is the greatest gift you can give them.

Chapter 19

Recognizing the Narcissist (Saying No Again)

Discipline

"The greater danger for most of us lies not in setting our aim
too high and falling short, but in setting our
aim too low and achieving our mark."

— Michelangelo

Even though I had spent twenty years with two life-sucking abusers, I thought I had finally figured life out. I was becoming aware of the games people played, but I was battling to rewire my thinking. I kept falling into the same rabbit hole. I guess you could say that each relationship taught me I deserved a better life. Each taught me valuable life lessons, and I became stronger for each experience, but I was still trying to find myself.

I spent time with my AA family, and I learned about building healthy friendships. Our group went camping on Hurricane Ridge, skydiving in Shelton, Washington, and celebrated holidays together. Many of us were just trying to find our way, and I was grateful for some of the members who had been sober for many years. I am blessed that even though I tried to disappear, I reconnected with a couple of them, and we reminisced over lunch a few times.

As I struggled to improve my confidence and independence, I fell into yet another mind-numbing trap. The difference this time was that I rented a room in his house for a few months. By then, Emma and Roger had grown up, graduated, and moved out. I was living alone with the remnants of two broken relationships, and I found I was constantly trying to pick up the pieces. I was looking after a sweet, chocolate Labrador named Charlie, but he spent a lot of time alone. I found Charlie a new home, rented out my house, and went back to school. I worked on my associates degree in arts and sciences while working full-time. The college campus was forty minutes from my house, which is why I rented it out, and moved into a studio apartment. I was burning the candle at both ends between school and work.

I met another man who started trying to run my life, but the way he did it was so subtle it appeared he was helping me. He bought me gifts and let me drive his fancy Corvette. I did not know how to feel. When we made a deal to move my double-wide mobile home to a piece of land he was connected to, everything changed. The land was a beautiful, forested two-and-a-half acres about twenty minutes from where I worked. I thought living there was perfect.

But then it happened. We had a contract for the land because my credit had been destroyed, and I needed help getting the land. My mobile home was almost paid off. Like I said, then it happened. Once again, the mask he wore came off, and I saw his agenda. Up until that point, we had a platonic friendship. After the land deal, he wanted more. At one point, he said, "Why do you think I was helping you all this time?"

I was so angry. But this time, it was different because everything had been between friends, and now, he was demanding a relationship. I strongly said no and returned to my house.

With this last disappointment, I decided my life with men was over. After all, I kept getting lost in the Machiavellian mindset of the men I attracted. I had initially joined Alcoholics Anonymous (AA) because I thought I had a problem with alcohol. What I have realized over the years is that alcohol was not the problem. The problem was I lacked the skills to cope with life, and I did not have the ability to assess the people who entered my life. AA was how I met my former land partner. So once again, I rented out my house, and even though I continued to work at the same job, I went into seclusion. In many ways, I fell off the grid. No cell phone, no internet, no address. I was trying to pick up the pieces of my pathetic life, and I had put most of my belongings into storage. I felt broken, and no one would even notice my absence. I was so ashamed, embarrassed, and emotionally shattered. The thought of suicide entered my mind a few times; however, I am a firm believer that every life is a miracle and has a purpose. Who am I to think for a minute that I should consider destroying myself?

Focus Questions

1. Was there a time you considered hurting yourself? Describe it.

---

2. What caused you to reach that point?

_____

_____

_____

_____

_____

_____

3. What actions did you take?

_____

_____

_____

_____

_____

_____

4. Why are you grateful today that you were not successful?

_____

_____

_____

_____

_____

_____

Summary

It is hard to keep trying to judge people's characters when you keep making the same mistakes about them. But disciplining yourself to recognize others' unhealthy behaviors is critical. Watch people carefully, and don't be too quick to give of yourself. We all have times of frustration when we reach a point of wanting to give up. But those are the critical moments to discipline yourself to keep going and learning. Never give up on yourself!

Chapter 20

Picking Up the Wreckage of My Life

Tenacity/Courage

"Always keep moving forward."

— Mutti

My maternal grandmother, Mutti, was such an inspiration to me during my difficult marriage. In 1987, she was sitting in her pickup truck in a parking lot waiting for her husband Isa to return from the store. Some young boys were setting off bottle rockets near her vehicle. The explosions startled her, and she had a heart attack. Remembering her time during World War II, as the bombs were dropping in Tallinn, I can only imagine how she felt at that moment. Her heart had been severely damaged, and later that night, she had a massive heart attack and passed away. I was devastated that it happened so fast, and I couldn't see her one last time. I was thirty-four and trying to file divorce papers at that time.

My mother spent time every day trying to help my step-grand-father Isa. He had a difficult time adapting to living alone in their home. We later learned that he spent most of his time burning all the letters Mutti had received from friends in Estonia and Germany.

His mindset evidently was still to protect those he loved from the Russians and Germans. Sadly, he passed away in 1989 with heart complications. I think in some ways he died of a broken heart. Mutti and Isa never saw their homeland liberated from Russian occupation.

During this time, I was struggling with many difficulties. I had filed for divorce after fourteen years of domestic violence. I found myself raising two children alone and struggling with money. I had severe panic attacks, sought comfort and courage in alcohol, and had been ordered into counseling. But my salvation came from a source beyond counseling and an alcohol rehabilitation program. My driving force came from remembering my grandmother's journey to freedom during World War II. We all have someone who displays indomitable spirit. Who was your motivational role model?

One night, I was settling into bed when my departed grandparents came to visit me. They were wearing the same clothes they had been wearing when we buried them. I could see them clearly, yet I could see through them to the picture hanging crookedly on the wall. They looked like holograms. No one uttered a word, but we communicated through our minds, telepathically. Their messages were in Estonian. They answered all my questions as if I spoke them out loud. They helped me understand everything I needed to know.

I have no idea how long they were with me, but I sensed that if I reached out to touch them, they would have to leave. I tried hard not to reach out, but I yearned for my grandmother to hug me or even just hold my hand. During all my difficulties, I had always asked myself, "What would Mutti do?" She was my rock, my courage. After all, she had separated from her husband during World War II and brought her two young daughters out of Estonia while bombs were being dropped on their city.

As I mentioned early in my story, in March of 1944, as World War II pressed on, my mother was thirteen years old. One day, she was in her father's apartment in Tallinn warming milk on the stove. Her mother, Mutti, came to the apartment with travel papers for Ella, Mom's younger sister; Mutti and Ella were leaving for a friend's home in Germany. Mutti told my mother she had to stay with her father because she could only get travel papers for one daughter. My mother ran out of the kitchen, leaving the milk to boil over on the stove. She begged and cried, saying she could not bear to stay with her father. She clutched her mother's legs and kept begging as tears rolled down her face. She said her father treated her very badly. My grandmother saw the fear in her daughter's eyes and made a risky decision. With bombs dropping on the city, she told my mother to quickly pack a few belongings. Mutti took both daughters, and the trio embarked on their dangerous journey to Germany.

During World War II, the German Luftwaffe and Soviet Long Range Aviation forces bombed the Estonian capital city of Tallinn on several occasions. My father later described to me the massive orange glow hovering over the city of Tallinn. He could see the colors of the devastating destruction in the sky from his island farm on Hiiumaa. In an effort to debilitate Germany, Tallinn was targeted several times for bombings by Soviet forces.

As my grandmother guided her two daughters through the rubble, nothing was recognizable. Everyone carried cardboard suitcases and random bags of assorted clothing, valuables, and documents. The trio hurried through the rubble with bombs dropping in the distance.

My mother heard a baby cry. She called out to Mutti, "Stop! We must help the child!" Mutti sternly said, "We must keep moving!"

This tragic moment left an indelible mark on my mother's heart, and the memory would haunt her the rest of her life.

My mother's sister Ella was only seven years old. At times during their escape, Ella became hysterical. My aunt would silently struggle with the memories her entire life.

Many a night, my grandmother would leave the girls at a bomb shelter. They would try to sleep, watch over their bags, and wait. Mutti would leave for several hours, but she never said where she had been or what she had been doing.

Mutti and her daughters cautiously navigated through the devastation on their way to the train station. In their exhaustion, they were unable to cover the distance. Little Ella could no longer carry her share of the bags, and when she saw a truckload of German soldiers sitting next to the roadside, she became hysterical. Mutti positioned Mom along the side of the road with the suitcases and bags. She looked back over her shoulder to check on Mom one more time. I can only imagine what she was thinking as she carried her screaming youngster into the woods to calm her down. Mutti saw the German soldiers sitting and talking on the other side of the road. Mom sat quietly, with her head down and eyes focused on the ground. She could hear the men speaking in German and laughing. She understood enough German to know they were talking about her. They laughed that she was merely a skinny young girl of no use to them. Years later, Mom told me she was grateful she hadn't physically developed yet. When Mutti returned carrying a subdued Ella, they finally resumed their trek to the train station. Their journey had taken several difficult days of walking, but they had finally completed the first segment of their road to safety.

As they boarded the train and settled into some vacant seats, the conductor was gathering tickets and checking documents. My mom didn't have any documents or even a ticket. When the conductor approached them, Mutti stepped into the aisle and walked to the end of the train car with the conductor to discuss their situation. The girls waited in nervous silence, holding hands. When Mutti and the conductor returned, the conductor softly spoke to the frightened young ladies. His words brought reassurance. "You have been through so much that your journey to Germany is approved. May you have a safe and pleasant journey to your new home."

The weary trio could finally rest. They were on their way to Mittenwald, Germany. Mutti had a friend who had offered them safety in her home. Mutti would later relocate with her daughters to Sweden.

As I shared earlier, the heaviest of the air assaults was on March 9, 1944. On May 10, 1944, my father and five other brave young men escaped on a small boat. They navigated successfully across the treacherous Baltic Sea, arriving on the coast of Sweden after almost twenty-four hours of brutal storms.

My father and grandmother are two of the most inspiring people I know. Their tenacity and courage through life-threatening situations taught me how important it is to stay in control of our minds. We cannot control what happens in our environment. We can only control how we choose to act with intent and move through the challenges.

Despite my best efforts to resist that night my grandparents appeared to me, I finally reached out, and within the blink of an eye, my grandparents were gone.

That was the first night in years that I slept soundly without any panic attacks. To this day, I have never had another panic attack. From that night forward, when I struggled with life choices, I always asked myself, "What would Mutti do? What would my father do?" My personal challenge was not World War II, but it was also a battle for life or death.

Tenacity is the quality or fact of being determined. My grandmother and father showed pure tenacity to survive and create new lives in a new country. Who inspires you with their true grit and tenacity?

With the guidance of Dr. Michael Gross and meditation, I am incredibly blessed to hear my father and grandmother's voices in the quiet moments. They continue to guide me through their loving energies of courage. I must also add that my mother showed incredible courage traveling alone to Canada. But when I hear her voice, she brings me comfort and grace, which brings me a balanced life.

Focus Questions

1. Do you have family members who inspire you? Explain who and how.

_____

_____

_____

_____

_____

_____

2. If you could go back in time, who would you want to spend a day with?

_____

_____

_____

_____

_____

_____

3. Why did you pick that person?

_____

_____

_____

_____

_____

_____

4. If you could give a younger you a life message, what would it be?

_____

_____

_____

_____

_____

_____

Summary

In our times of greatest challenge, I have learned that those who love us really do reach us through unconditional love. Love transcends all dimensions. We just need to have the courage and tenacity to trust our inner voice and believe what we hear. Remember, spirituality is your life experiences. Your soul is unique to you, so only you know what you feel and hear. Remember, faith is in the lack of evidence.

Chapter 21

Be Careful What You Pray For

Faith/Loyalty

"If you wish to reach the highest, begin at the lowest."

— Publilius Syrus

At one of the lowest points in my life, I would occasionally stop into a late AA meeting because I knew I didn't want to use alcohol as a crutch anymore. I knew other people had happy lives and loving families. I wanted that too! My pride and ego stopped me from reaching out to my parents for many reasons. The biggest was I didn't have the courage to face my father. I was not ready to hear him say, "See, I told you that would happen." My self-worth, self-love, and self-esteem were crushed. The only thought that kept coming to me was to start praying again. I had turned away from my faith for many reasons, even though I still believed in a Higher Power. Now, my whole life was hanging on by a thread.

My advice to anyone who can relate to this is: Be careful what you pray for. Clearly, my needs were massive, but in my heart, I just wanted a friend. I will always remember the night I got down on my knees in a vacant parking lot. As I looked up to the heavens, cool rain fell on my face, flowing down my cheeks with my warm tears. To the best of my ability, I put my trust in God, as I understood our Higher Power back then. As the night's chill began to make my body hurt, I found a blanket and curled up to sleep in my car. When the sun began to warm my cheek, I found a local gas station and washed up and prepared for a full day at work. I was grateful I had a small income to keep me in gas and food.

After a busy day at work, I decided to go to an AA meeting. I entered the room of a small office building, poured some coffee, and found an empty chair in the corner. Yes, I put on my strong face. I didn't want anyone to see how broken and alone my soul felt. The meeting was like most meetings—uneventful; we just sit and share our stories. I spoke a little, but I spent most of the meeting listening to others. I noticed a quiet, gray-haired man sitting across the room in another remote corner of the room. I saw how intently he listened to me as I shared my story.

During the meeting, a woman shared that she had recently lost her mother to cancer. She was having a difficult time sharing how she felt. I decided to invite her to a local restaurant for coffee and pie after the meeting. As we all congregated outside, I learned the woman's name was Sue. We agreed where we would meet.

I saw the quiet man standing in the distance across the parking lot. He was standing alone and appeared lost. As a long-time AA member, I felt the urge to invite him to join us for coffee. When I called out the invitation, I watched his face light up, and he began to smile and walk over to us. My heart filled with warmth because I saw his grateful smile. I told him where we were going to meet, and he agreed to join us.

As I headed for my car, he politely asked if he could walk with me. I smiled and nodded. I was still feeling the warmth around my heart when he asked if he could drive me to the restaurant and we could come back for my car later. I am not sure why I agreed, but it was only a few blocks away, so I thought it would give me a few minutes to get to know him a bit. Through my friends in AA, I have learned that when you reach a low point, you need to find someone you can help. The unsourced phrase I heard many times is, "When you are upset because you have no shoes, remember the person who has no feet and remain grateful."

When we got to the restaurant, Sue had already found a table and was looking at the menu. I introduced her to Ken, our new friend. As we settled into our chairs, we listened to Sue as she told us about her mother. At one point, Ken began to tell us he had recently lost his wife to Crohn's Disease. I knew then that was why we were all brought together. They were both dealing with losses. I was so glad we had the time together, and I thought the two of them might become friends. I had absolutely no idea what was about to happen.

At the end of the evening, as we left the restaurant, I gave Sue a hug, and we agreed to talk again soon. Then Ken drove me back to my car.

Ken was a complete gentleman. When he parked the car, he ran around to open the door for me. I was so surprised. Then he asked if he could call me. I dropped my head, embarrassed to tell him my phone had been disconnected. The only number I had was my work phone, and we could only accept emergency calls. He didn't know I was almost homeless. That was my secret. Embarrassment filled my soul. I felt so humbled after such a nice evening having coffee with friends.

I was shocked by what Ken did next. He handed me a tissue for my tears, reached into his other pocket, and handed me his cellphone. He said, "Now you have a phone, and I already know the number." I was overwhelmed by his genuine kindness, but I told him I could not accept his generous gift. He barely knew me; who knows where I would call? He reassured me he knew me well enough, and he knew I wouldn't take advantage of his gift. I kept the phone, and we began talking every night before we went to sleep.

We were both struggling with empty nests. We were alone and our children had moved away to begin lives of their own. I had prayed for a friend, and my prayer had been answered. One thing I have learned is that when we pray, we cannot have any expectations. Ken did not fit the image of a friend I had prayed for, but he turned out to be so very much more than I could have ever imagined.

Never have expectations when you ask God, the True Source, for something. In my loneliness, I was expecting someone younger with small children and a secure job. But God answered with a caring, good friend, seven years older than me, with gray hair, a nicely trimmed beard, and a dark-brown moustache. His thinning hair was pulled back into a ponytail, and his eyes were kind. He had two adult daughters, one married and the youngest planning her wedding.

Clearly, our paths had crossed for a reason, and we began meeting after work. One day when we were talking, Ken invited me to move into his house. He knew my living situation was challenging at best, and he was reaching out to help.

Ken told me he had a three-bedroom house with lots of room. He told me I could have my own room, rent-free. My life was a mess, and I was broke, so free sounded good. Before I could stop myself, I accepted—but with many restrictions.

I was not ready for an intimate relationship with anyone, but I seriously needed a friend I could trust. After all, I had made an ugly mess with my life. I thought about the offer overnight and decided it was worth a try. I believe intuition led me to my decision.

In March of 1997, I packed all my worldly goods (that were not housed in storage) into my car and met Ken in town. After a bite to eat at a restaurant in Silverdale, Washington, we headed up the hill to his house. I had never been to Seabeck before, and I followed him down a long road, which turned into another long country road. As the miles passed, I wondered if I should make a U-turn and head back to town. But something inside compelled me to keep following him. The road meandered through the forest, past a lake and a couple of little gas stations. When he finally slowed down and turned left, my heart jumped.

Ken was leading me up a long dirt road, into the forest, up a hill, then down the other side of the mountain. I honestly thought, *"Oh, heck, this guy is a chainsaw murderer, and I am in so much trouble."* But even with all my fears, I kept driving behind him. At that moment, I paused and remembered that God, the True Source, would not leave me now, not after everything I had survived. I held on tightly to my faith, believing I would be safe.

Before we left town, Ken had told me he would park alongside the house so I could park in front. I still cannot believe how trusting I was after everything I had endured, but he was so very kind. There was truly something different about Ken.

As I saw Ken's car making the final turn into the driveway, I took a deep breath. We were deep in the forest and there were no other houses in view. I was a bit apprehensive because I was alone with a man I barely knew. As I saw the house for the first time, the motion of his car triggered the light to illuminate the driveway. It seemed like a comfortable, secluded home. His Old English Sheepdog, Sadie, came off the front porch to welcome me. I sighed with relief as Ken offered to help me unload my car. We put the boxes in a spare bedroom. He showed me around the house and said, "Welcome to my humble home."

As I came up the stairs for the first time, I saw plants, a beautiful rustic essence, and beautiful antiques mixed with bamboo furniture. He had pictures of his daughters when they were young and framed newspaper clippings of his life with his beautiful wife. I could feel the love within the walls of his home—and the new emptiness. It was a truly difficult change in his life. My heart hurt for him and his loss.

I walked around with mixed feelings because I saw so much of his dear, deceased wife around the house. Clearly, they had been a happy family, and he was struggling with her loss. She had died only six months earlier. We both needed a friend, and this began a new life journey for us.

Ken had no idea who he had invited into his home, and for a long time, I felt like he could not be for real. He was such a hardworking, quiet man, and I was such a chatterbox. He was careful with his finances, secure in his job, and focused on retirement.

It took me a long time to adjust to living with someone so different from the men I was familiar with. Ken was nothing like anyone I had ever met, and in the early months, I kept waiting for the "other shoe to drop." For the first few years, I kept thinking I must be living in a dream. I had no idea I would be worthy of such a beautiful love. Yet, twenty-four years later, we are still together. Yes, we are opposites in many ways, but we come from different lives, which is how many relationships begin. New relationships are created as we weave our life tapestries together. We bring many different memories and lessons together into a beautiful creation of dreams woven together with golden threads of love.

My life has truly been blessed since Ken began helping me pick up the shattered wreckage. It has taken me years to grow out of toxic thinking, low self-esteem, and so much more. His loving patience has brought me through so many challenges. We have had our differences, but he has continued to stay consistent in his actions, and he has never raised a hand to hurt me. He has called me on my toxic thinking and insecurities. His methods have been challenging because he made me face things I have been running away from most of my adult life.

With a narcissist, you never know what to expect. When I was married, I had to expect the worst so I could be prepared.

Living with Ken is very different because he is consistently a kind, caring man. He has given me so much more than a comfortable home in the mountains. He has taught me, he loves me, he respects me, and more than anything, he supports my ideas and encourages me to face my fears and discover my true self. Ken has encouraged me to become confident and make decisions for myself without asking for permission from him or anyone else.

We have helped each other through many challenges. When we met, we each had two children, and in the following few years, we both became grandparents. I have two grandsons, and Ken has one grandson and two granddaughters. Our families have blossomed, and our friendship continues to grow.

Had it not been for Ken's encouragement and support, I may never have gone on the journey to find my true self. He supported my decision to move to Arizona, not once but twice. When I was paralyzed with fear and stopped along the roadside, he came to me and encouraged me to continue my journey. I could not believe how strong he was when he reminded me that I needed to keep following my heart or I would always regret my retreat. Never once did he try to stop me, even though I knew his heart was aching, wondering if I would return.

I was like a boomerang in the early days. In our twenty-four years, we continued a long-distance relationship for ten years, with the daily phone calls and meeting up a few times a year. I was trying to find myself, and Ken knew I needed time to understand my greatest potential. When challenges came into my life, Ken was always there for me. It felt like Ken was my brother in the way he always stood by me, never judging, just making suggestions.

People come into our lives all the time. Sometimes they grace us with joy, laughter, or lessons, and then they move on. But other people become lifelong companions, and our lives are enriched by their presence. Those are the people we put in our inner circle and have a special love for. If they are ever in need, we will do anything to protect and help them. Those friends are rare, so if you have one or two, consider yourself incredibly blessed. I am honored to have two friends who enrich my life in my inner circle. I will introduce the other a little later.

I moved to Arizona because I needed a change from my job, and my daughter Emma had recently given birth to my first grandchild. I remember what it felt like to be a new mother, and I wanted to help and bond with our newest family member, my grandson.

When I met him, I was awed and would sit and just watch him as he slept in his crib. The miracle of life is such a blessing and should always be celebrated and appreciated. It is truly an honor to be a grandparent. In a way, perhaps, I saw his birth as a gift to me for enduring so much heartache.

Focus Questions

1. Describe someone who gives you moral support.

_____

_____

_____

_____

_____

_____

2. Describe a time you struggled with trusting people.

_____

_____

_____

_____

_____

_____

3. Why are there times you ask for permission to do something on your own?

_____

_____

_____

_____

_____

4. How would you bring a blended family together?

_____

_____

_____

_____

_____

_____

5. If you had the opportunity to create your perfect life, what would it be like?

_____

_____

_____

_____

_____

_____

Summary

When we feel restless, we often struggle because we feel like something is missing. Perhaps we have preconceived ideas of what our perfect family should be like. Many of us find our self-worth, self-love, and self-esteem when we get others' approval. But what we fail to realize is we should not be seeking others' opinions. When we lack confidence and are seeking approval, we need to look at why we are not trusting ourselves. Granted, through years of abuse, it's easy to doubt yourself, but that's when you need to look in the mirror and remember your own strengths. Think about all the challenges you have overcome. You are stronger than you think you are, so give yourself credit for that. It's time to be true to you and have faith that you will find balance and harmony in your life.

Chapter 22

The Many Places
I Have Searched

Fear/Courage

"Use your fear…it can take you to the place
where you store your courage."

— Amelia Earhart

In 2001, I settled into my new life in Arizona, I struggled to find a sense of belonging. Most of my coworkers were involved with their families, friends, and churches. Today, I know why I felt out of place.

While living in Arizona, I focused on my health, joined a gym, began lifting weights, and trained for the San Diego Marathon. Over the next ten years, I became a homeowner and full-time college student while working full-time.

But I was still searching for the one thing missing from my life. I had no idea what I was looking for, but I felt my life, albeit very complete, still needed something more. Nothing I learned or achieved filled the void in my soul.

Mixed in with the positive goals, my life was peppered with several surgeries, which I considered challenges to conquer. Some of my injuries were due to pushing my body too hard. Other surgeries were the result of injuries during my years of abuse. My life was a constant progression of five steps forward, four steps back with recovering. But I learned that even small steps forward are in a positive direction.

In retrospect, my lifetime search continued through all the activities I included in my busy life as a new grandmother. While a full-time employee, I became a full-time college student. I earned my Bachelor of Science Degree in Human Services and Management online. I completed the San Diego Marathon, and challenged myself to drive across the country on a 5,400-mile road trip to Dallas, Texas. For someone like me, who had been deathly afraid to drive ten miles to a grocery store alone, I realized the hardest part of that journey was driving the first few miles away from home. My travels continued with an adventure to Cabo San Lucas, Mexico, a road trip to Calgary, Alberta, and trips overseas to Estonia, Sweden, France, and The Netherlands.

My dear friend Ken gave me so much moral support and encouragement while I was trying to find my purpose in life. I called him many times in tears because I was afraid of something.

In 2008, I was far from my narcissistic ex-husband Walter, and I was looking for my purpose. I decided to join a mission trip to Cameroon to build shelters for AIDS orphans. I put the wheels in motion, completing the needed paperwork, getting travel shots, and putting my documents in order. But as the time approached, with my bag packed, I started getting cold feet and nervous nausea. I called the trip coordinators and expressed my fears. My heart wanted to go, but my fears were crippling me.

My apprehension began when I returned from work one day to find the side door of the house open and my house in shambles. Devastated, and scheduled to leave for Africa in a few weeks, I began doubting myself again. I felt violated because it was my first real house purchased on my own—a large, four-bedroom. This was not a mobile home. I think my silent warrior came out as I furiously entered my house. I grabbed a baseball bat, hoping I would catch the thieves in the act.

Seeing all my cabinets and cupboards opened with my stuff gone or destroyed on the floor made me angry. My television set, mountain bike, cameras, photography gear, heirloom jewelry, various tools, and other items were gone. I was crushed!

The police who came to take a report were very cold and formal. They see this type of thing so much that to them it was routine, not a big deal. But it was very disturbing to me. Picking through all the precious family pictures strewn on the floor hurt my heart, but it reminded me that we all began with nothing and the things stolen or destroyed had only been things, no matter how sentimental they might be.

In hindsight, it was a good thing the thieves were gone. Unfortunately, the worst thing the thieves took was my sense of safety. Despite all the years I had lived alone in that house, I could no longer sleep in my bedroom. I installed alarms and new safety doors, but my peace of mind was gone. My living room became my sleeping quarters because it was centrally located, and I could watch all the doorways. Many a night, I slept on the floor, guarding my home.

The mission leaders in Florida assured me I would receive a few days of training with the other members of the mission team. Many people voiced similar concerns because of our remote destination in Cameroon. I did my self-talk—I had come so far, knew I would not be alone, and the group was a faith-based group. We were on a mission to share the Word of God, the True Source, and help build a rescue unit in the village of Ngie.

I searched within my heart and reminded myself that this was the journey of a lifetime, so if I fell victim to my fears, I would always regret it. On the day of departure, I locked every door and window in my house and double-checked that they were secure, then grabbed my gear. As I rode out of my driveway, I remember thinking my house had already been robbed, so there wasn't much left to take, and it was just stuff. The only things important are family pictures. Everything else is replaceable. My journey to Africa was beginning, and I refused to wallow in fear. It would be one of the most incredible adventures of my life! Some words of wisdom from a dear friend in AA came to mind: "Take baby steps toward your fears…one day at a time."

I followed his advice, and when my nerves kicked in, I told myself I just needed to get to Florida. Once there, I was shy and quite the loner, but we were partnered up with people for training sessions and projects, allowing us to get acquainted. It was important to build relationships before we embarked on our long flight to Paris and onto Cameroon. I made a few friends, whom I am blessed to still be in contact with today.

The night before we left for the airport, I called Ken in Washington State. I will never forget how scared I was. I stood on a walkway, listening to frogs, and when I heard his voice, I began to cry into the phone. The reality of the mission trip hit me. Even though we no longer lived together, or even in the same state, he had become my trusted friend and we spoke on the phone every night.

Ken's voice gave me comfort, but I was terrified of the journey I was embarking upon. Once again, he came to my rescue and reminded me how far I had come. He said I shouldn't give up now because I would regret that decision. I can only imagine how he felt hearing my trembling voice. But I knew he was right, and I had to honor my commitment and not give in to my fears. I pulled myself up by my boot-straps. I told Ken how much I loved him, and how grateful I was for his constant support. Truly, everyone needs a good friend like Ken. He has been an answer to my prayers since the day we met.

I am thankful that I beat my fears. I knew I wouldn't be able to talk to Ken for three weeks. I only hoped I'd be able to call him from the airport in Paris. Internet access where we were going would be sparse, and the only communication we could make was to let our families know we had arrived safely.

As we boarded the largest airplane I had ever been on, our team was scattered. Our mission team leaders were already at the headquarters in Douala, Cameroon, awaiting our arrival. During a short transfer in Paris, France, I made a quick call to Ken (we would have time during our return trip to spend a day in Paris before returning to United States), and then we boarded our flight to Douala, Cameroon. My greatest memory was flying over the Sahara Desert! The sands looked orange as the sun beat on the endless rolling hills. The desert was as vast as the eye could see and showed no signs of life. There is life in the Sahara Desert, but none we could see from our altitude. The vastness was greater than any land I had ever seen.

After several hours in flight, our jet finally landed at Douala International Airport. After thorough customs inspections and baggage checks, we gathered our team. We departed the airport, and our team was ushered to a bus waiting near the exit doors. Our gear was loaded onto the bus, and we were asked to board quickly. It was February and very warm in Cameroon. We were warned to keep our bags in our laps and not to put our hands out the open windows.

I learned very quickly why these instructions were needed. Once we got settled on the bus, a throng of people started reaching out and leaning on the bus, trying to get whatever they could get their hands on. They spoke predominantly French and a little English; they were asking for money and anything we had. The bus began to roll away with people still hanging onto it. I had never experienced anything like it before.

The hoard of needy people faded into the distance as the bus headed for the mission headquarters. I began to wonder what I had gotten myself into, and I could see other members of our team were concerned as well. We were relieved to see a high wire fence surrounding the mission headquarters compound.

We were met by the team leaders. Our gear was unloaded, and we were told what was expected of us. We were escorted to a small, simple sleeping area and had a chance to clean up. Then we walked to a local restaurant for a delicious meal.

Focus Questions

1. What have you done that was terrifying?

_____

_____

_____

_____

_____

_____

2. Describe the outcome and how you conquered your fear.

_____

_____

_____

_____

_____

_____

3. How did someone give you moral support and encouragement?

_____

_____

_____

_____

_____

4. How did that person's actions make you feel?

_____

_____

_____

_____

_____

Summary

Facing your fears is scary, but many people miss the most beautiful part of their life journey because they do not face them. They sit undecided and watch opportunities and adventures slip away. In the end, they live a life of regrets. Those who face their fears will find their courage and some of the greatest blessings of their life.

"The graveyard is the richest place on earth, because it is here that you will find all the hopes and dreams that were never fulfilled, the books that were never written, the songs that were never sung, the inventions that were never shared, the cures that were never discovered, all because someone was too afraid to take that first step, keep with the problem, or determined to carry out their dream."

— Les Brown

Part IV

Becoming My True Self

Chapter 23

Introduction to The Inner Voice

Discipline

"We must all suffer one of two things: the pain of
discipline or the pain of regret and disappointment."

— Jim Rohn

You have read through parts of my story, from childhood to
being a teenager in the 1960s and a young mom in early 1970s. My
life has zig-zagged across the continent, and at times, to Europe and
Africa as I have searched for my purpose. Today, my adult children
have families of their own, and I find myself looking forward to the
best part of my life. Yes, my life has been challenging, but it molded
me into the person I am becoming now. This point in my life re-
minds me of this simple cliché: "The past is gone. The future has not
arrived. We just have this moment in time. Nothing is guaranteed."
Okay, maybe death and taxes.

Through every challenge I have faced, the one thing I believe in
with steadfast conviction is my inner voice. Some people call it listening to your gut or intuition, but no matter what we call it, when
we listen to that guidance, things go far better than we could have

imagined. Life is not a dress rehearsal. Everyone is given one chance to live their life and reach their greatest potential. The problem is that many of us are stuck just like I was—sacrificing ourselves for the benefit of others because we love them. That is a noble task, to be sure, but at what cost to yourself? We spill blood, sweat, and tears for our children and aging parents, and we justify our actions, believing we do things because we love them. Many times, our compassion, understanding, and loving empathy are not returned, and we feel used and empty.

As mentioned earlier, our soul is remembering and learning through our experiences. It makes us who we are. We are all an aspect of God, the True Source, and we are created from unconditional love. Being of love and giving love to others is what we all do. But so often, we become so busy that we forget to love the most important person in our lives—ourselves!

When I first heard this idea, I felt it was an arrogant concept. In my list of priorities, I had placed my needs after the needs of everyone else I loved. But that is a big mistake so many of us make. We cannot teach what we do not know, and we cannot pour from an empty cup. This simple analogy makes this point crystal clear. On airplanes, we are always instructed to put on our oxygen mask first, then assist our children to put on theirs.

As I share my journey from the swill under the gutter to the beautiful, overwhelming feeling of unconditional love, I have finally learned to start accepting who I am. When you begin to connect to and understand your true self, you discover your soul and the beautiful, loving person you truly are. Everyone has a story, and it really matters little where you come from. What matters is that you are perfect within yourself right now, and when you begin to love yourself, you grow ever more perfect and begin to radiate a more loving energy from within and out to the world and people around you. People will be drawn to you because your energy is positive, and nothing negative can survive in the energy of love.

JUST BE YOU—JUST LOVE YOU—JUST TRUST YOU

Yes, it is easy to say, "Just be you," but it is one of the most challenging things to do. We are so focused on being successful, comparing ourselves to others, and providing for loved ones that there seems to be little time in a day to focus on our needs. Healing heartaches begins by bringing them out and looking at them for what they are. What part did you play in the event? You must take responsibility for only your part, not the whole thing. Look at it, understand it, and release that painful energy. It is so important to love yourself. But you need to learn who you really are, your passion, and your mission and goals.

To begin healing your heartaches, you must bring them out of hiding, look at them, understand them, forgive the person who hurt you, and consider your part in the event leading to the pain. Only then can you finally learn and release the pain. The memory will always be with you, but it will only be a reminder of what you endured and how you became better for the experience. Hold onto the lesson and let the heartache go.

Good advice, right? Now how in the world are you supposed to do it? Well, I will tell you how I finally learned to release the most painful heartaches, but first I must share something else with you.

This is such a valuable golden nugget that I feel it is worth repeating. Through the course of your life, your soul has felt all your emotions. Your soul, also known as your higher self, knows what you have been through. Every time you were abused, betrayed, got bullied, or heard negative comments about yourself, a piece of your soul was torn away and went into hiding somewhere deep within your core. As you grow and live an adult life, those pieces of your soul remain hidden. Your self-worth, self-love, and self-esteem continue to diminish. But you continue to function because your family depends on you. What happens over time is more and more of your soul tears away and you become more bitter and driven by ego. You placate your feelings with material things like new cars, fancy homes, new clothes, and trips to luxurious locations. The reality is that you are trying to find a sense of personal value.

The caveat is you cannot take any of that with you when you depart this life. The only thing of value you can take is unconditional love. Which brings me back to my point: When your soul is in hiding deep within your core, you continue to grapple with stress and challenges. Your doubts, fears, and insecurities are like a parasite that eats away at your emotions and your body, and it can manifest itself in physical illnesses, aches, and pains—even panic attacks.

As a survivor of long-term domestic violence and abuse, I had no idea how to handle stress. My coping tool for stress was alcohol. As I mentioned before, alcohol was liquid courage for me while I was being abused. After I decided to stop drinking, AA was my family. But what I failed to realize is I had no idea how to survive in the real world. To create self-worth, self-love, and self-esteem, one also needs to exercise self-discipline. Consuming alcohol or comfort food irresponsibly establishes patterns that are difficult to overcome.

Focus Questions

1. When you are going through a stressful situation, how do you cope?

_____

_____

_____

_____

_____

2. How do you comfort yourself with food or alcohol?

_____

_____

_____

_____

_____

3. Do you have a group of friends you trust who support you with comfort or advice? Describe your support team.

_____

_____

_____

_____

_____

4. When facing challenges, describe how you cope.

_____

_____

_____

_____

_____

Summary

People cope with stress in many ways. But we need to discipline ourselves to use positive skills. We need to remember we are responsible for our own decisions. At the moment we are most vulnerable, we fall prey to the influences of others. Remember, you are in control of your decisions; trust your intuition, your gut instinct, or just listen to your inner voice. I fell into self-medicating with alcohol; it was my liquid courage to go home in the early days of abuse, but alcohol was a poor choice for many reasons. My suggestion is to decide on your healthy coping skills. Prepare them. Have a call list of people who will be your hotline network, take a hot bath, or partake in an activity. Then when you feel stressed, you already have a plan for what you can do to handle it. My support network became my Alcoholics Anonymous family. AA often uses the following Serenity Prayer to assist in healing:

God, grant me the serenity
to accept the things
I cannot change;
The courage to change
the things I can;
and the wisdom to know
the difference.

— Reinhold Niebuhr (1892-1971)

Chapter 24

Arizona, Washington, Canada

Love/Truth

"There are only two energies on this planet.
Love and anything that is not of love. Become Love!"

— Dr. Michael Gross, T.S.

The ebb and flow of life's energies takes us on interesting journeys. I faced many challenges as I adjusted to life on my own in my beautiful house. I was finally beginning to enjoy my life. Yes, my house was robbed, but I refused to fall victim to my fears. It was robbed three weeks before I went to Africa and then robbed again, the following year. The insurance company warned me that burglars have a pattern. The first time they enter, they assess what you own, knowing you will replace things. They often target your home for another robbery. I continued to build my fortress, or so I thought, but even new security doors did not deter the thieves. After months of sleeping on the floor or in my recliner, I had to overcome my fears and begin trusting that I would be safe. It was a victory in my personal growth when I finally returned to sleeping in my bed.

Then it happened! One night, while relaxing before bed, I felt a strong pressure in my chest. It was not like a heart attack or anything, but I had to take a deep breath. The feeling I experienced was the urge to move back in with Ken. I had retired from my job and was looking forward to finally spending more time discovering Arizona with my grandsons. Yes, I had two by this time. I was recovering from surgery on my shoulder due to injuries from an auto accident. I decided not to consider the move back to Washington because I was really beginning to enjoy my new life as a retiree. Healing was going well, and I was returning to my gym.

But the feeling kept getting stronger, and I had to consider life with my grandsons or life with Ken and being closer to my aging parents, who lived in Victoria and were in their eighties. I could feel the squeeze of the sandwich generation. They were still living in the house I had walked away from in 1972. The saying "Life goes full circle" kept running through my mind. As much as I tried to fight the urge, because I loved being with my grandsons, I had to consider these might be the last years with my parents. I was struggling to decide between going after my dreams and listening to my inner voice. After much contemplation and discussion with Ken, I finally made the tough decision to return to Washington.

I remember the last time I drove up to Emma's house to say goodbye to everyone. My little red pickup truck was fully loaded, and the rear bumper was sagging low to the ground with the weight of my worldly possessions. I sold what I could, donated what I could, and stored some big pieces of furniture with my good friend in Arizona. Ironically, his name is also Ken. We had become good friends through all my packing adventures, and he was the recipient of some of the furniture.

It was getting late on that hot spring evening, and my grandsons were running around in their underwear. After a short visit, I gave them each a huge hug and felt the tears welling up in my eyes. I quickly turned so they would not see my tears as I hurried to the truck. In one final look back, I saw them doing a crazy dance in the doorway as we waved goodbye.

With a heavy heart, I began the long drive back to Washington. I kept telling myself it would be fine; I would be with Ken and closer to my son Roger. I needed to make one more stop before I began the long drive. I had to see my Arizona Ken. We met at our favorite casino for a bite to eat and a little time together chatting and trying our luck. As we sat at a couple of slot machines, his machine began to make all kinds of noises—he had hit a sizeable jackpot. While he was waiting for a slot agent to confirm his winnings, my machine also began making noises. It was a nice way to end the evening.

Oddly, when the slot agent gave me my winnings, she said, "You have a long journey ahead, and you will need this." This woman could not know my truck was fully loaded for an out-of-state move; neither Ken nor I had said anything to her.

But as I began to put miles on my odometer and Arizona disappeared into the horizon, things happened. Thinking back to seeing my grandsons dancing in the doorway, I began to cry. My heart was breaking. I believe I cried most of the way across the Mojave Desert.

Now, I had learned long ago that coincidences are God, the True Source's way of staying anonymous. As I drove through the Mojave Desert, my truck began pulling to the right. I wondered what was happening because I had recently bought new tires and had everything on my truck checked in preparation for the long road trip. As

I drove up the infamous Grapevine, I stayed in the slow lane because I had to drive slower than most of the traffic.

My little truck performed like the little engine that could up the hills of the Grapevine. At one point, unfortunately, I had to pass a very slow-moving semi-truck. The moment I changed lanes, I hit a big pothole, which shifted my steering a little more to the right. At the top of the hill, I noticed an exit—perfect! I saw a coffee shop and gas station, so I thought I would check the load and the tires. It was also a good time to call Ken in Washington to let him know where I was. He tracked my progress so that if I had any problems and didn't call, at least he would know roughly where to start looking for me. It was a safety thing we always did when I was traveling alone.

When I called Ken, he suggested I check the oil. When I reached in for the dipstick, I noticed a bubble bulging out of the inside of the front right tire. I knew right away that was the reason my truck had been pulling to the right. I told Ken what the problem was, then hurried inside to ask the store clerk where I could get a tire changed. He told me if I hurried, there was a place across the highway, but it closed at 5:00 p.m. I only had five minutes to get there.

As I hustled back out to my truck, I saw that a large, white pickup had parked so close to my driver door that I could not get back into my truck. A man was sitting in the passenger seat, so I hurried around the white truck to ask if he could move the vehicle. Then I saw "Roadside Service" painted on the door. When I asked if he could help me, the young man said, "We are off work now, but my dad's coming out, and you can ask him."

I was totally relieved when the older man agreed to help me. They did more for me than I expected. They not only changed my tire, but they rotated my tires because I had a little donut spare tire, not suitable to be the load-bearing tire. The older man told me it was a good thing I had stopped when I did—a chunk of rubber was missing from my tire and only a thin layer of rubber was holding the tire together. Had it blown, my truck would have gone off the highway.

The tire I had was purchased at a store in Arizona. Coincidentally, just a few exits along the highway was another store that carried the same tires. I followed the information, paid the two men from my casino winnings, and got a hotel near the tire store.

After a good night's sleep, I took my truck to the recommended tire shop and explained what had happened. The store manager looked at my damaged tire and told me he could tell by the tread that it was still very new. After a short wait, my truck was ready to get back on the road. When the manager explained my bill, I was happy to hear the price was only half what I had expected. Again, the casino winnings covered the costs. The slot agent had been right in her comment. Was that coincidence?

I took one side trip to San Francisco because I had no idea when I would have another chance to explore the city. I wanted to drive my truck down the crookedest street—Lombard Street. Now, I must confess, I am quite a "seat of the pants, spontaneous adventure seeker." Seldom do I plan scheduled trips because, as a photographer, it is so easy to get distracted and lose track of time. This adventure was also a random decision. It is how I have lived most of my life.

In driving down the most crooked street, what I failed to consider was not only the narrow width of the street but the angle of the slope. My truck was fully loaded, and the rear bumper was barely one foot above the ground. The higher up the hill I drove, the more upward the front end of my truck pointed. I could hear the rear bumper scraping the roadway. I honestly do not know if my front tires became airborne, but as I drove ever so slowly, all I could see was the beautiful blue sky. Finally, as my eyes were wide open, and a little prayer was running through my head, the front of the truck slowly shifted, and the next thing I saw was the steep grade of the hill's downward side.

The view was breathtaking, or perhaps it was the entire experience that was breathtaking. One night in San Francisco and I was hooked. The city has so much to see. Fisherman's Wharf would have been interesting to explore, but another time, another trip. It was time to continue north. I drove across the Golden Gate Bridge and stopped to be a tourist and take photos. I could see Alcatraz in the distance and put it on my must-see bucket list.

My long journey continued uneventfully, with a few rest stop/ photo shoots. As I pulled into Ken's driveway, I noticed he had carved my name into a wooden sign hanging next to the front door. As he stepped out onto the porch, arms wide open, he said, "Welcome home." What a beautiful way to begin a new chapter in my life. I knew enough time had gone by since we had struggled with empty nests, and now, we were finally looking forward to a life together. We had both retired, and it was time for us to enjoy our golden years.

The magic golden moments lasted two days!

Early the third morning, the phone rang. It was my younger sister, Margaret. She was living close to our parents and worked in a nursing home as a registered nurse. Frantically, Margaret told me our father was in the hospital, and I needed to come help her. Our mother's dementia was getting worse, and someone needed to be with her.

I threw some clothes into a bag and told Ken I had to leave. He understood, and I will always remember him saying, "Next time you come for a two-day visit, don't bring so much stuff." We had spent the last day unloading all my boxes out of the truck.

I share this story because in the first year that I returned to live with Ken, many things happened. It was hard to sell my house in Arizona and leave Emma and my grandsons, but what lay ahead was why I needed to be in Washington. My father was diagnosed with prostate cancer and needed surgery. My mother had progressed to full Alzheimer's and had wandered off before I got there. Fortunately, a police patrol found her walking aimlessly in her nightgown in the early morning hours, looking for my dad. She could not remember he was in the hospital.

In the fall, my father's sister was succumbing to pancreatic cancer. My father and I traveled to Toronto for our final visit. At that same time, my mother had fallen several times and was in the hospital on a locked floor so she could not wander off. She was soon in a nursing home, and five months later, my father and I were with her as she took her final breath. Three months later, my mother's sister also passed away while undergoing kidney dialysis.

Had I ignored my inner voice, I would have been in the wrong place to help my family. With all the challenges I've faced, I know how important it is to believe and trust my inner voice. That inner voice—I call it my soul—is guiding me to my destiny.

I will share with you now the gift I received by listening to my persistent inner voice.

Excerpt from my upcoming book: *Believing in Love Again*

A Mother's Love

The room was dimly lit by two small night-lights. The glow from a streetlight also shone into the window. She was lying on the bed covered by a green, fleece blanket. I did not recognize the blanket and barely recognized my sweet mother. She was like a pale, frail shell of herself.

I could hear people talking in the hall. Some of the staff were trying to get another elderly resident to bed. I closed the door to quiet the noise. It was my turn to spend the night with my mother. We had been advised that since she could no longer swallow food, her time would end within seven days. My father and I both felt like we were watching her starve to death. But we were advised by the nurse in charge that with Alzheimer's, my mother had reached a point where she could no longer swallow. To feed her would cause her to choke, and it would be very distressful for her. My father and I were doing a 24/7 bedside vigil because we could not bear to leave her alone.

I know my mother loved to hear Louis Armstrong sing, so I was playing "It's a Wonderful World" for her. She had not opened her eyes or spoken a word in days. From time to time, the nurses would come in to turn her to her side and check her vitals. She was on her back, and as I stood beside her bed, I could see her time to leave this world was getting close. If I had anything to tell her, true confessions or just sharing love, it had to be tonight.

When the nurse left, I began my apologies for running away and not being a better daughter. I told her how much I loved her and admired her courage. On and on I spoke. Mom was incredibly close to her mother, Mutti, and I had wished we had been more like that in our relationship. But when I was nine years old, my mother got sick, and I became her caregiver until she recovered from surgery.

After talking for a long time and shedding a few tears, I just wanted to hug her. I had been afraid to hug her frail, small body for fear of causing her pain. She barely weighed 100 pounds. But I knew it would probably be my last hug. She had slid down into the fold in her hospital bed, and I was unable to get the railing down, so I climbed across the foot of her bed.

I gently reached down to put my arms around my mom, knowing her arms would not hug me back. I was shocked to feel her bones through the blanket as I gently embraced my dear, sweet mother. I cradled her in my hug and softly whispered, "I love you." My mom didn't move, but to my surprise, her eyes slowly opened. They were a beautiful, brilliant blue, like I remembered from when I was a little girl. She looked at me, recognized me, and with all her effort, she said, "I...love...you...too!" She used all her energy to say those precious words to me.

My heart melted. Her eyes closed, and through the tears streaming down my cheeks, I gently put her back down on the bed. I climbed off the bed and pulled the blanket up over her shoulders, saying, "I know you used to always stitch the sheet to the blanket, but I don't have any thread." My voice quivered as I spoke softly to my mother.

I was trying to stop crying when the nurse walked in. She could see my tears and asked if I was all right. At first, all I could do was tremble and wipe away my tears. After I swallowed hard and collected myself a little, I told her what had just happened.

I described how hard my mother had worked to say each word, almost like she had to get the strength to speak. She was so weak that she could not even hold up her head. Yet she had spoken to me! The nurse smiled, gave me another hug, and said, "You just had a shining." I knew nothing about a shining, but I do know it was my mother's final gift to me. Years later, it would be a treasured memory that would help me endure the challenges that lay ahead. I kept that treasure safely tucked in my heart, never telling anyone until right now, telling you.

> "Love is our true destiny. We do not find the meaning of life
> by ourselves alone—we find it with another."

> — Thomas Merton

As my mother took her last breath, I whispered in her ear my promise to take care of my dad. He was stoic through all the preparations, and I could feel his sadness. They had been together more than sixty years. I created a photo mural project to honor their life together. As we worked on the project together, he began sharing stories about their lives in Estonia, before they met in Sweden. We talked, laughed, and I witnessed his love and joy when he shared stories of their adventures in Sweden, where they had met.

My dad and I also spoke about his last trip back to his home in Hiiumaa. He had built a beautiful home on the land where he was born. The land carried such a legacy, and I was honored to walk with him on his last walk. His knees were painful, so we walked slowly and he sat to rest when needed. Despite his comments, I brought his walker, and he was glad he had a place to sit. He shared what it felt like to return to the farmland and reminisce. I saw the softer side of my father in these special moments. I saw the man my mother loved.

Sometimes, our parents wear masks because they want to appear strong to us. I know now that their stoic expressions protect us from their heartaches. I can only imagine how my father was feeling when we laid my mother to rest. At the graveside service, I stood beside him. He leaned against his walker holding a red rose; his eyes teared up, but he never shed a tear. He remained strong for his daughters.

When it was my father's turn to join my mother, I held his hand, gave him my love, and reassured him I would be all right. Now, my parents are together again, perhaps dancing in heaven's garden.

Today, I know "Love transcends all limits." I continue to feel my parents' love and embrace their energies in my dreams. I am honored to have been with both of my parents when they took their last breaths. Listening to my inner voice led me to the right place at the right time. Had I ignored the persistent feeling, everything would have been different.

Focus Questions

1. How do you define the meaning of life?

_____

_____

_____

_____

_____

_____

2. Describe what you believe happens after someone passes away.

_____

_____

_____

_____

_____

_____

3. Have you experienced the loss of a loved one? Describe how you felt.

_____

_____

_____

_____

_____

_____

4. What did you learn from that loss?

_____

_____

_____

_____

_____

Summary

As mentioned, before we are all energy and nothing negative can survive in the energy of love. We are made of love, in a moment of supreme love, and love is the glue that keeps us together. I have learned that when life in this world ends for people, their souls continue to exist in another realm; you could say another dimension. Their energy of love transcends all limits, and I shared a little of my experiences in that. I must stress how important it is to trust your inner voice. Be open to learning more about spirituality because it truly is the beginning of your greatest love story. When you have to make difficult decisions, take a moment and ask your heart/soul what you should do. You may not get an answer right away, but when you do, trust that message and watch how your life begins to change. Always lead with a loving heart and know you hear the truth.

Part V

Gratitude and Spiritual Growth

Chapter 25

From Gutter to Amazing Grace

Gratitude

"What a precious privilege it is to be alive—
to breathe, to think, to enjoy, to love."

— Marcus Aurielius

After traveling back to Estonia several times after my parents died, I knew they wanted me to share their beautiful love story. I began writing *Believing in Love Again* to honor them and leave a legacy for my children and grandchildren. Their stories are powerful, and I feel if I don't share them, they will be lost forever. As Abraham Lincoln said: "The written word is the only way the dead can speak to the yet unborn."

While early in the process of writing my book, I was invited to hear Patrick Snow, international best-selling author, professional speaker, and book publishing and marketing coach, speak at an event. Interestingly, he shared the same quote from Abraham Lincoln. Today, I am honored to have Patrick as my writing coach.

My life had been going well, or so I thought. Time had passed since the loss of my father, and I became involved in Taekwondo.

I was spending time with my best friend, planning activities, and talking about trips to visit our children and grandchildren. My life challenges were few and things were comfortable. But part of me felt restless, like something was missing. I had no idea what I was seeking, but today, I know I was looking for my purpose in life. After so many decades, I knew even though my life was so much better, I still yearned to find the missing piece—the piece that would put all the stories and experiences I have shared in this book together. I have been told there are no accidents in life. Clearly, when I was born and my parents called me their accident, the words hurt, but it made me believe I was here for a reason. My rollercoaster life had a purpose, but I still needed to find out what it was.

In 2019, after a trip to Estonia and Sweden, I returned home to share my experiences with my writing coach, Patrick. I had seen visions of my parents as young adults in some of the places I visited in Sweden. As I told Patrick about my experiences, he encouraged me to contact someone who has become the greatest blessing in my life. Patrick spoke very highly of Dr. Michael Gross, author of *The Spiritual Primer*. I was shy and uncertain, but I felt the need to speak with Michael. At first, I tried to ignore the feeling, but the urge to call him was so strong that I arranged a time to meet and buy his book. Patrick had praised him so highly that I felt the pressure in my chest nudging me to meet this inspiring spiritual coach.

Finally, in October 2019, I decided to call Michael and we met at a restaurant in Gig Harbor, Washington. I was inspired by his peaceful presence and engaging wisdom. The meeting was very enjoyable, and I was excited to begin reading *The Spiritual Primer*. I will always remember how honored I felt to be in his company, and I was thrilled that he signed my copy of his book.

It is truly a treasured moment when someone enters your life, awakens your soul, and reveals the missing piece you have been searching for your entire life. I am eternally grateful that Michael has come into my life because he has taught me how to rise above the gutter of domestic violence and abuse to embrace my life of amazing grace. My self-worth, self-love, and self-esteem are blossoming, and I am on the most incredible journey. We are never too old to grow into our higher selves.

Opening the Universe

"There's no darkness around you
only the light in your Soul.
Let the light out."

— Dr. Michael Gross, T. S.

As I mentioned, the day I met Michael, I knew my search was finally over. I had no idea what would be revealed, but for the first time, all the puzzle pieces were beginning to fall into place. I had been raised learning about God in church, and that concept has always been within me. But I kept feeling like something was missing. As a young adult, I often attended different churches because we had moved a lot, and I was still searching for the missing piece. I kept feeling like something was not being taught. There were times when my mind wandered to this thought: We should be holding church services outside, and the buildings should be secondary. After all, Mother Earth is the most majestic place of gathering.

I began reading *The Spiritual Primer*. But when I realized it was also a workbook, I put it aside and did not do the exercises. I just kept reading random parts. After reading a few chapters, I began doing the exercises. By then, I had highlighted many parts and dog-eared many pages. About three months after reading the book, I knew I would need to work with Michael. It was another compelling feeling in my gut, you could say. But I knew it was something important I needed to pursue.

On the first visit, we agreed to meet at his home. He graciously welcomed me and all my questions. When I first stepped into his home, I felt a calming sense of peace. For the first time in many years, I truly felt like I was safe and away from negativity. Finally, I no longer felt like I was being watched and judged. It felt different than anything I had ever experienced. I was apprehensive and curious. He offered me a cup of tea, which I gratefully accepted. As we began getting acquainted by sharing a bit of our stories, I began to relax. It was January 10, 2020, and I was about to begin my most incredible journey of awakening my soul.

Each day, I know many blessings have been unfolding in my life. The missing piece was revealed when Michael answered my question, "What is the difference between religion and spirituality?" He answered that religion is taught by the written word, such as the Bible. It sets a moral code. Spirituality is your life experiences, unique to you. The things you know are true in your mind, and if you told those experiences to anyone else, they might not believe you.

All the pieces of my fragmented memories began to make sense. I started meditating every morning before I began my day. As a night person, retired and no longer facing demands of my day to wake up early, it was customary for me to sleep until 9:00 a.m. or later. When I began meditating, I woke early, meditated, and returned to bed. But so much has changed, and now I wake up at 5:00 a.m., count my blessings, and meditate. My morning always begins with gratitude and positive attitude, and I look for ways to follow my true purpose.

As I mentioned before, I have searched for my purpose my entire life. In high school classes, I would gaze out of the window, wondering what I wanted to do with my life. After thirteen years in school, my free spirit, hippie soul did not want to go to college. My father had offered to pay for my college if I went to the local university and studied nursing or learned to be a secretary. Neither option appealed to me. As a certified nurse's assistant, my experience in nursing was limited, but I already knew my stomach would be my downfall. Many times, when providing patient care, I fought the urge to vomit and become another patient.

Most of my life, I was under the impression that being a wife and mother would be my purpose. To me, being a mother was the most precious gift, and I treasure it to this day. What I did not realize back in the early days of motherhood was that we truly only share our lives with our children for the first eighteen years. We teach them the life lessons we know to help them with their futures, but there comes a time when they leave the nest and begin lives of their own. Obviously, I knew my children would leave home. What I didn't realize was how hard that part of their life would be. We need to respect that and watch them as they grow and discover their way in life.

Life is not linear. It is ever-changing as a multi-dimensional energy. Understanding that has helped me realize my children have their own families, and as my grandsons grow up, we continue to evolve as a family in harmony and balance, with unconditional love.

God, the True Source, has aligned my life with Dr. Michael Gross for an important reason. I will continue repeating how grateful I am that Michael has worked with me so diligently that I have been able to rise above the swill and heartache of my past and finally embrace the power of unconditional love. It does not matter what others teach or how others think; what matters is what you think and feel. My purpose is unfolding as I write these words. Michael continues to help me understand my life experiences, and he helps me continue to grow spiritually. What I have been seeking most of my life has been inside me all along. On some level, I knew it was inside me. But I had no idea how to understand and allow my soul to grow. Michael has led me into a journey of inner growth. Through his guidance, I have been able to rise above the gutter where I fell during the many episodes of abuse. I have faced many painful memories, cried oceans of tears, and wanted to walk away from this journey many times. My spiritual journey has brought me face to face with my fears, and I have felt the fight, flight, or freeze emotions many times.

With consistent coaching from Michael, I am finally becoming the loving, caring person who has been within me my entire life. You could say my true self went into hiding, and now I am beginning to blossom. Conquering my past, forgiving those who have hurt me, and being grateful for the lessons I am learning is far, far greater than any vision I could have had for myself.

Sometimes, life takes us down challenging roads, and we make poor choices. We learn, we grow, and ultimately, our goal is to reach our destiny. Our higher self is guiding us through intuition and gut feelings. We are all aspects of God, the True Source. Created in love, of love, and unconditionally loved. Our greatest mission is to love the person we are and give love to others.

When I began rising above the wreckage of my life, I started to feel a sense of empowerment. No longer am I a victim of my past; now I am a victor and creator of my future. Reflecting on my past through writing this book, I remember feeling lost and broken. But the memories bring forth new strengths in my warrior soul.

It is my belief that *yes*, those who love you feel your love on the other side, and it comes back to you ten-fold. Remember, we cannot share that which we have not experienced. But I share this because I have been blessed to feel tremendous unconditional love. The details of this experience are very personal, but I will just say the overwhelming love from the other side has taken me to my knees in tears of joy.

Feelings of resentment and anger toward the people who have hurt you must be released. To move through the emotions of domestic violence is very hard, but the rewards to you will be enormous when you begin to forgive and find gratitude for the lessons you have learned through the relationships. Those events will always be a memory, so hold onto the lesson and release the heartache and pain. As you find your way through the memories, you will grow stronger in self-worth, self-love, and self-esteem.

One thing that was revealed to me after thirty-four years away from abuse was that I was still living in a prison of fear. Even though the door was open, I was still trapped inside by my own fears. After so many decades of emptiness, I finally began to let the True Source lift me out of the negativity and back into unconditional love in the real world.

Life truly does come full circle when you believe. At first, I did not want to move back to Washington. It was like returning to the memories of hell, but then I realized a home is not a place in the outer plane. Home is where the love is, where your soul and your true self are waiting for you to wake it up. Thanks to Michael, I found what I have been searching for my whole life: Me!

Yes, my life has been peppered with many challenges and blessings. But I would not change anything I have experienced. Everything good or bad has filled my soul with an abundance of life experiences, which has led me to understand my mission and goal. I have said this many times, "It doesn't matter where you begin in life. What matters is the person you become along the way." Which brings me back to my heritage: The Nine Noble Virtues from the Viking Era. My life experiences have also led me to adding six additional virtues, which are the foundation of:

15 Steps To Your Freedom

COURAGE – TRUTH/HONESTY – HONOR – FIDELITY/
LOYALTY – DISCIPLINE – HOSPITALITY – GRATITUDE –
SELF-RELIANCE – PERSEVERANCE/TENACITY – LOVE –
INTEGRITY – TRUST – FORGIVENESS –
RESILIENCE – CURIOSITY

Focus Questions

1. Have you had a spiritual experience? Describe it here.

_____

_____

_____

_____

_____

_____

2. Did you tell anyone? How did they respond?

_____

_____

_____

_____

_____

_____

3. When it comes to faith, do you feel like something is missing?

_____

_____

_____

_____

_____

_____

4. Have you experienced déjà vu? Describe your experience.

_____

_____

_____

_____

_____

_____

Summary

One of the greatest healing techniques I have learned is gratitude. It is important to be grateful to the people who have hurt you because you have learned valuable lessons through the experiences. Through meditation and understanding your spiritual experiences, you gain a greater understanding of how your energies are affected by emotions. Once you begin to forgive, you allow gratitude to enter your life. We cannot change the events of the past, but we can change how we handle ourselves. As we become grateful for the lessons we learn and thank our abusers, we improve our self-worth, self-love, and self-esteem. That also raises our soul's vibrations to where we become more loving.

A sense of empowerment occurs when you feel a shift within your soul. Your former self releases negative energies, allowing your soul to grow with the beautiful energy of unconditional love. As your soul reunites with your physical body, an incredible sense of peace and love pervades.

How many times have you been told "Just be you"? It seems like a simple question, right? But as you honestly try to answer, you often cannot seem to get past your own ego. Many say ego stands for "Edging God Out." But for a long time, my former self thought, *I am not sure there is a God.* Why would some people like me suffer so much while others were enjoying luxurious lives? The answer is within you. Begin to listen to your inner voice—I like to call it soul talk—all your life experiences are within you. When I began to listen, I realized that God, the True Source, has always been with me. Through all the abuse and violence, when I almost gave up, my inner voice kept telling me, "Get up! Get up! Get up! You are not a quitter, and this is not your destiny."

Chapter 26

Forgiving Your Abusers

Forgiveness

"True forgiveness is when you can say
thank you for the experience."

— Oprah Winfrey

In looking back upon the challenges that I have faced, it is easy to point fingers of blame. But blaming others for the choices I made is nothing more than side-stepping my own responsibility. I have no control over how other people behave, but I do have control over how I act. This is easy to discuss now, but the lesson came at a great cost to many of my family members.

Standing up to my father was a moment of independence, perhaps defiance. As I walked away, I felt proud but also sad. I knew at that moment that I did not want anything to do with my father, but I knew my mother would hear his rage. It would fall upon her shoulders to calm him and reassure him he was still a good father. They still had one young daughter at home they needed to raise. Perhaps the third child would be the charming moment of glory they had hoped all of us would be at one time.

I choose not to linger over guilt or anger. Through my tears, I looked forward to the adventures that lay ahead for my new independent life. Decades of nervous fear, panic attacks, and heartache would pass before I would experience the power of forgiveness. In time, I found a deeper understanding of how people show love. It's not always easy to see. By understanding how my father was raised, I began to see how he showed his love for me through his strict discipline and structure. I remembered how stoic he was when he saw my sweet mother, the love of his life, pass away. Through his strong exterior presence, I saw his heart breaking in his eyes. The process of forgiving my father and others who hurt me has been a long healing process. But it has opened my heart to also forgiving myself.

Forgiving yourself is just the beginning of the healing process. Understanding our mindset and that our thoughts influence our inner energy is an important part of improving self-worth, self-love, and self-esteem. Your belief in yourself improves when you uncover your hidden treasures, your passions. Remember your passions fuel your soul.

"We are what we think…
All that we are,
Arises with our thoughts.
With our thoughts we make our world."

— Buddha

This quote from Buddha encapsulates one of the greatest lessons I take with me from 2020. Personal growth comes from within. As you begin to pay attention to your thoughts, answer these questions.

Focus Questions

1. Are your thoughts positive or negative? Write some examples.

_____

_____

_____

_____

_____

_____

2. How do you praise or judge other people?

_____

_____

_____

_____

_____

_____

3. How do you feel when someone compliments or criticizes you?

_____

_____

_____

_____

_____

_____

4. Are you seeking approval? What do you do?

_____

_____

_____

_____

_____

_____

5. Are you genuinely happy for others' success, or are you jealous? Give an example.

_____

_____

_____

_____

_____

_____

Summary

Our energies ebb and flow through life with a variety of vibrations and frequencies. Just like music resonates within your body, so do your emotions. Our goal is to raise our vibrations through positive, loving actions. Dr. Michael Gross teaches that we need to retrain our brains. Pay attention to your thoughts, and if you find that you are expressing negative thoughts, incorporate this simple phrase into your thoughts. Begin saying out loud "5-4-3-2-1 Cancel, Cancel, Cancel." This simple phrase interrupts your thinking, and since there can be no vacuum in the universe, replace your thoughts with something positive. If you don't replace the negative thought with something positive, the negative thought will return. I use simple phrases like "I like ice cream." You'll begin to notice how often you think negative thoughts, and in time, you will begin to put more positive energies around you. With positive and loving thoughts, you will find your way to forgiveness.

In many ways, my life has come full circle. I currently live geographically close to where I lived when the domestic violence escalated in 1986. It was never my plan to return to what I referred to as "My Hell on Earth." But returning to the Pacific Northwest, I have found myself returning to the many scenes of attacks by three different abusers. However, it is evident that returning to this area was exactly what I needed to do to understand the lessons yet to be learned.

You have read parts of my story, from childhood to being a teenager in the 1960s and a young mom in early 1970s. You have followed my life as it zig-zagged across the continent, and at times, to Europe and Africa as I searched for my purpose. Today, my children are adults with families of their own, and I find myself looking forward to the best part of my life. If you were to ask me, "What would you change?" my answer would be, "Nothing!" Yes, life has been challenging, but it molded me into the person I am becoming now. "The past is gone. The future has not arrived. We just have this moment in time. Nothing is guaranteed." When you thank your abusers and forgive yourself for the choices you made, you experience your greatest healing and growth.

Today, our world continues to be in chaos due to the coronavirus pandemic. There is uncertainty and many mixed emotions. How we grow through these times is contingent on our own mindset. As I mentioned earlier, everything is energy. Our words, our emotions, and our actions all create either positive or negative energies that spread. Stay mindful and share positive and loving energies through your thoughts and actions.

"Always remember to forgive yourself for any
mistakes you have made and
forgive others for their mistakes.
The purpose for doing this is to free
yourself of anxiety and emotional pain so
that you can always move forward."

— Dr. Michael Gross, T. S.

Chapter 27

The Answers Are Within You

Unconditional Love

"What you think you become. What you feel you attract.
What you imagine you create."

— Buddha

We often hear the cliché: "Everything you need in life is inside you." Have you ever really given that much thought? Dr. Michael Gross taught me about the "Veil of Forgetfulness." Our souls choose to incarnate in our bodies so our souls can learn and experience life's lessons. Our soul remembers everything about our life and what is ahead for us. The purpose of life is to awaken our soul, understand what our mission is, and follow our passion, whatever that may be.

Perhaps you know your mission. Perhaps you are a doctor, a scientist, an artist, a teacher, or an author. For the longest time, I just wanted a secure job so I could provide for my family. It was frightening for me to become an entrepreneur and be my own leader. I lacked self-worth, self-love, and self-esteem. Knowing that I had settled for a position working with the government, I never allowed myself to find my greatest potential. After almost thirty years, I had spilled blood, sweat, and tears for a company that only knew me as a number.

As the years progressed in that job, I denied myself one of the most important positions of all. I was a single working mom, so I lost years of quality time with my children. I have always considered them the most important people in my world, followed by my parents. As it is for most people, family is important to me, and at times, I still struggle with guilt from knowing I could have been a better mother, better daughter, and better sister. But I remind myself that I have always aspired to do the best I can. It was my honor to be with my mother when her soul went to a greater garden in 2011. When my father went to join my mother in the gardens of heaven, I held his hand as I heard his last breath. At that moment, with the words, "I love you," I released him. He will always be with me!

In retrospect, one thread has continued through my challenging journey. At my lowest points, when I had nothing left, I heard the thoughts of my soul. Through my tears of desperation, I listened, continued to rise above abuse, and am alive today to help other lost souls find their way. Through meditation and the guidance of my spiritual mentor, Dr. Michael Gross, I see how my destiny is unfolding. There is no greater blessing than the awakening of a lost soul.

"Listen to the still small voice within, for in it,
God, the True Source, speaks."

"Freedom Begins Within!"

— Tiiu Napp, T. S.

POINTS TO REMEMBER: You Are Worthy!

1. Proclaim your rarity.

2. Remember your roots, your heritage.

3. Let go and just be you.

4. Listen to your inner voice.

5. Reclaim your pen and write your own story.

6. Everything you need is inside you.

7. You have free will and can change your mindset.

8. Choose your words wisely.

9. Just be *love*!

10. Love will heal—unconditional love is the glue that will *Heal the Holes in Your Soul.*

A Final Note

This Moment in Time

"In the process of letting go you will lose many
things from the past but you will find yourself."

— Deepak Chopra

Who you were at twenty is not who you were at thirty, and who
you were at thirty is not who you are at forty. As we move through
life, we continue to change. Life is peppered with wins and challenges. As I have heard many times, the past is over and the future
has not arrived—all we have is this moment in time. What if there
is no tomorrow? Will you look back on life and have regrets, or will
you look back and know you did your best and enriched lives with
unconditional love?

Healing the Holes in Your Soul is my life story, and I hope something from it resonated with you. We are all made of love. Out
of millions of possibilities, we were brought into this world for a
purpose. Dr. Michael Gross opened the vast universe of spirituality to me, and it was the missing piece to the puzzle of my life.
I count my blessings every day that, after a lifetime of searching
and enduring tremendous abuse that tore away pieces of my soul,
today I know how to understand the challenges and accept them

with grace and gratitude. Each challenge brings forth a new lesson, which makes each one of us stronger and more loving to those who do not understand.

Everyone has challenges, and every soul feels pieces tearing, but everyone has the answer within themselves. I speak from experience, and together, we can begin *Healing the Holes in Your Soul.*

Conclusion

The Great Awakening Begins

The Beginning of the Greatest Love Story of All

"Love is the only energy that can never
be extinguished, only set aside
but always there."

— Dr. Michael Gross, T. S.

The "Great Awakening" begins within. All the people you have loved who have passed away are living energy within you. At times, you may hear their laughter, smell their fragrance, and feel the warmth of their love. They have left an indelible piece of their essence within you. What you admired in them becomes qualities you also carry. God, the True Source, has created us as an interwoven fabric of life. We are created and interlaced with unconditional love on many levels.

Everyone has a soul mission and goal, but very few really listen to what their soul thoughts are. I am incredibly honored to be on my spiritual journey, experiencing incredible places and the power of unconditional love that fills every fiber of my body, deep within my core. Love really does transcend all limits…. It is unlimited!

Reflecting on the stories I shared, I realize many times the trajectory of my life could have gone in a far better direction had I followed my inner voice. Life is not a linear journey; it is the ebb and flow of energies moving among a multitude of dimensions through many vibrations and frequencies in the universe. Our mind, body, and soul are all energies, and it is up to us to live in harmony and balance within our bodies and with the energies on our planet. Emotion is an energy, as I mentioned earlier, and when you decide to follow your soul, there is no vacillating or indecision. When Dr. Michael Gross began working with me, my life experiences began to make sense, and I could finally begin the process of letting go of the pain and heartache of so many challenges. By releasing the negative energies and finding forgiveness in my heart, I began the process of healing with unconditional love.

When I understood I am in control of my life and my decisions, I finally became the master of my life. Today, I write my own life story, and no one will ever take away my pen again. One early morning when I was meditating and asking God, the True Source, for clarity on my life mission and goals, Spirit told me, "Follow your passion; it fuels your soul." It took me a few minutes to connect my memories, but this is how my thoughts aligned.

- Photography has been my passion since the day my grandmother gave me my first camera. It was a Brownie camera, and I think I was eight years old.

- My grandmother inspired me through my many episodes of abuse and domestic violence.

- In my meditations, I often hear my grandmother's voice. At the lowest point in my life, she came to visit me with my grandfather. They appeared like holograms standing by my bedside. Since that night years ago, I have not had a panic attack.

- After my ex-husband was finally out of my life, I had no idea what to do. My counselor told me to go to a mall, a bookstore, and just walk around to see what attracted my attention. Again, I found myself in the photography section. I began a freelance side job in photography. I was incredibly shy, but my camera was my shield. I witnessed weddings, celebrations, and life through the lens of the camera. My camera was my courage and my extra income through challenging times.

- Up to this point, my thoughts were lining up like a time-line of my life in the outside world.

- Here is the sweet spot! I remembered all the nights I spent in my makeshift darkroom, the time I spent on photo shoots, the nights I missed sleep because I lost track of time—they were all because of my passion for the art of photography. It was never about the money. I often gave away photography for free. Some of my pictures are published, and yes, I was a finalist in a contest that took me to Universal Studio in California, where I met the famous actor Betty White. But I am sharing this with you because, even though I have known this for a long time, as with many things, it had been buried under the muck of life.

- When I took another look at this memory, I realized the greatest return on my photography has never been the money but the joy, the happiness, and the love that the images bring to others. Every precious moment when I give someone a photograph, big or small, I watch their eyes. In those precious moments when I feel their love, captured in that image they are holding, their emotions fuel my soul.

• When we enrich our soul by following our passion, we improve our self-worth, self-love, and self-esteem. Isn't that what life is all about? Healing the holes in our souls truly begins within. You have everything you need to create a beautiful life; it is waiting inside you. All you need to do is begin to look within and find your passion.

• Your passion is the one thing you will get lost in doing. You will look forward to it, probably lose sleep doing it, and perhaps forget to eat, but you will be immersed in your richest world.

When you discover your life purpose and passion, nothing will stop you from pursuing your goals. It is not about money or success. It is about what you love to do, and you will be driven to do it. Perhaps your passion is music, cooking, or creating art—it doesn't matter what it is because it is your unique passion! Whatever it is, when you share it with others and see and feel their joy, it feeds your soul! You are changing the quality of not only your life but the lives of those you help. Always be of service to others. Our soul mission and goal is to gain self-worth, self-love, and self-esteem. When our passion fuels our soul, the unconditional love heals the holes, and we begin our incredible love story.

Congratulations on your "Great Awakening."

15 Steps to Your Freedom

When you go through the following steps in your soul's evolution, you will experience life the way it should be by experiencing true freedom.

1. Finding Your Courage

2. Upholding Truth/Honesty

3. Respecting with Honor

4. Practicing Fidelity/Loyalty

5. Maintaining Discipline

6. Exercising Hospitality

7. Applying Self-Reliance

8. Persevering through Tenacity

9. Living in Gratitude

10. Embracing Love

11. Maintaining Integrity

12. Understanding Trust

13. Healing through Forgiveness

14. Gaining Strength through Resilience

15. Living with Curiosity

About the Author

Tiiu Napp is an author, professional keynote speaker, transformational coach, entrepreneur, and survivor of domestic violence. She retired from a twenty-nine-year career as a rural mail carrier. Her past jobs include police radio dispatcher, extended care aide, freelance photographer, travel writer, salesperson, and marketer. As an entrepreneur, her multi-faceted network includes all-natural health products and how to create multiple streams of income through self-empowerment associations.

Tiiu has a wide range of interests that have led her to earning many certifications and degrees. She earned her Bachelor of Science in Human Services Management, graduating with honors from the University of Phoenix. Tiiu also earned an Associate in Arts and Sciences, from Olympic College, graduating on the President's List. She also earned several Service Awards from the United States Postal Service. Tiiu is a nondenominational ordained minister through The Church of Sanctuary. She has also earned a TEFL Professional Certificate from TEFL Institute and Certificate of Appreciation from the American Red Cross.

Following her inner voice, once she emerged from decades of abuse, Tiiu embarked on her quest of self-discovery. Her goal has always been to help others, and experience life from different perspectives. Her photography has been published in several issues of the *Photographer's Forum Best of Photography Annuals* and *Photography Vibes, Best of Edition*. One of her images earned her a page on the *Friskies Cat Calendar* and an opportunity to meet actor Betty White. She has traveled to a small village in Cameroon, Africa, as part of a mission team to build a rescue unit for AIDS orphans and worked locally on many community projects.

Tiiu has always had a passion for aviation, which led her to skydiving and flying small aircrafts. Her adventurous spirit has also taken her to earning her black belt in Taekwondo, and running 5Ks and marathons and climbing the stairways of tall buildings like the Seattle Space Needle and the Columbia Tower.

With such a variety of experiences, Tiiu's greatest achievement is her spiritual growth. She understands what it feels like to live in abuse, struggling for each breath of life. Tiiu understands the feeling of being paralyzed in fear, lacking the courage to call out for help. She has been called a victim, a survivor, a thriver, and an inspiration to others. Her "Never Give Up" attitude, her faith in God, the True Source, and her spiritual mentor, Dr. Michael Gross, have brought her into a life of unconditional love. Tiiu remains humble and honored to be helping others who are struggling with abuse and domestic violence. As an empath, she listens with compassion and shares how others can begin their journey to self-discovery and freedom. Tiiu shows how understanding your inner voice can improve your self-worth, self-love, and self-esteem.

About Tiiu Napp's Coaching and Healing

Tiiu Napp's mission is to help all those who have experienced abuse or domestic violence begin their journey to freedom. As you begin to work with Tiiu, she guides you from being a victim to a survivor and thriver.

By working with Tiiu, you will experience personal growth as you improve your self-worth, self-love, and self-esteem. She will customize "15 Steps to Your Freedom" specifically for you.

Tiiu believes everyone has a soul mission and goal in life. Even though life has brought incredible challenges to you through abuse and domestic violence, your life is valuable. It is Tiiu's goal to help you find your purpose, reveal your passions, and finally, find your life of abundance and unconditional love. Your journey to freedom begins within, and Tiiu will open the door to help you find your way.

If you wish to pursue your relationship with Tiiu further, she is available for consultations, coaching, emotional healings, and much more.

Reach out to Tiiu for a no-obligation, complimentary thirty-minute consultation by phone or in person if possible. She would be thrilled to chat with you.

480-223-7921 (private cell)
Text first name and time zone
Calls, visits, or Private Zooms can be scheduled.
tiiunapp3@gmail.com
www.HealingTheHolesInYourSoul.com

Book Tiiu Napp to Speak
at Your Next Event

When considering a motivational speaker for your next event, your choice is easy. Look to Tiiu Napp to grace your audience members with inspiring stories. She shares powerful messages that will have everyone wondering how she continues to bring joy and laughter through heartbreaking experiences.

No matter your audience's size or your location, Tiiu's passion will touch the hearts of everyone. Tiiu speaks from her soul because she knows what it feels like to be a victim of domestic violence. To rise above abuse and embrace a life of unconditional love is something everyone deserves.

Tiiu will engage, inspire, entertain, and encourage your audience members to look within and listen to their inner voices. She will leave your audience with valuable nuggets of knowledge and wanting more of her special energy.

Tiiu can speak to your group on topics such as how to:

- Overcome fear and find your courage.

- Recognize triggers.

- Understand learned behavior.

- Forgive your abuser and find gratitude.

- Be resilient.

- Understand how emotions affect your energies.

- Build self-worth, self-love, and self-esteem.

- Find unconditional love.

- Understand the thoughts of your soul.

- Listen to your inner voice.

Tiiu is honored to offer you a complimentary, no-obligation thirty-minute pre-speech interview. She looks forward to learning about your organization, its needs, and how she may help you.

480-223-7921 (private cell)
Text first name and time zone
Calls, visits, or Private Zooms can be scheduled.
tiiunapp3@gmail.com
www.HealingTheHolesInYourSoul.com